The Mexican Americans

Other books in the
Immigrants in America series:

The Mexican Americans

By Barbara Lee Bloom

LUCENT
BOOKS®

THOMSON
GALE™

San Diego • Detroit • New York • San Francisco • Cleveland • New Haven, Conn. • Waterville, Maine • London • Munich

LIBRARY OF CONGRESS CATALOGING-IN-PUBLICATION DATA

Bloom, Barbara Lee.
    The Mexican Americans / by Barbara Lee Bloom.
      v. cm. — (Immigrants in America)
Includes bibliographical references and index.
Contents: Life in Mexico—La raza—Working in *el norte*/the north—From open border to il-
legal immigrants—Communities in transition—Changing times—The Chicano movement—
Living the American dream—Blending old and new.
    ISBN 1-56006-753-5 (hardback : alk. paper)
     1. Mexican Americans—History—Juvenile literature. 2. Mexican Americans—Social con-
ditions—Juvenile literature. 3. Immigrants—United States—History—Juvenile literature. 4.
Mexico—Emigration and immigration—History—Juvenile literature. 5. United States—Emigration and immigration—History—Juvenile literature. [1. Mexican Americans.] I. Title.
II. Series.
    E184.M5B696 2004
    305.868'72073—dc21
                                                         2003010727

Printed in the United States of America

CONTENTS

FOREWORD

Immigrants have come to America at different times, for different reasons, and from many different places. They leave their homelands to escape religious and political persecution, poverty, war, famine, and countless other hardships. The journey is rarely easy. Sometimes, it entails a long and hazardous ocean voyage. Other times, it follows a circuitous route through refugee camps and foreign countries. At the turn of the twentieth century, for instance, Italian peasants, fleeing poverty, boarded steamships bound for New York, Boston, and other eastern seaports. And during the 1970s and 1980s, Vietnamese men, women, and children, victims of a devastating war, began arriving at refugee camps in Arkansas, Pennsylvania, Florida, and California, en route to establishing new lives in the United States.

Whatever the circumstances surrounding their departure, the immigrants' journey is always made more difficult by the knowledge that they leave behind family, friends, and a familiar way of life. Despite this, immigrants continue to come to America because, for many, the United States represents something they could not find at home: freedom and opportunity for themselves and their children.

No matter what their reasons for emigrating, where they have come from, or when they left, once here, nearly all immigrants face considerable challenges in adapting and making the United States their new home. Language barriers, unfamiliar surroundings, and sometimes hostile neighbors make it difficult for immigrants to assimilate into American society. Some Vietnamese, for instance, could not read or write in their native tongue when they arrived in the United States. This heightened their struggle to communicate with employers who demanded they be literate in English, a language vastly different from their own. Likewise, Irish immigrant school children in Boston faced classmates who teased and belittled their lilting accent. Immigrants from Russia often felt isolated, having settled in areas of the United States where they had no access to traditional Russian foods. Similarly, Italian families, used to certain wines and spices, rarely shopped or traveled outside of New York's Little Italy, a self-contained community cut off from the rest of the city.

Even when first-generation immigrants do successfully settle into life in the United States, their children, born in America, often have different values and are influenced more by their country of birth than their parents' traditions. Children want to be a part of the American culture and usually welcome American ideals, beliefs, and styles. As they become more Americanized—adopting western dating habits and fashions, for instance—they tend to cast aside or even actively reject the traditions embraced by their parents. Assimilation, then, often becomes an ideological dispute that creates conflict among immigrants of every ethnicity. Whether Chinese, Italian, Russian, or Vietnamese, young people battle their elders for respect, individuality, and freedom, issues that often would not have come up in their homeland. And no matter how tightly the first generations hold onto their traditions, in the end, it is usually the young people who decide what to keep and what to discard.

The Immigrants in America series fully examines the immigrant experience. Each book in the series discusses why the immigrants left their homeland, what the journey to America was like, what they experienced when they arrived, and the challenges of assimilation. Each volume includes discussion of triumph and tragedy, contributions and influences, history and the future. Fully documented primary and secondary source quotations enliven the text. Sidebars highlight interesting events and personalities. Annotated bibliographies offer ideas for additional research. Each book in this dynamic series provides students with a wealth of information as well as launching points for further discussion.

La Raza

The Mexican American people sometimes refer to themselves as *la raza*, a Spanish phrase meaning "the race," "the people," "our people." In the southwestern region of the United States, *la raza* has lived and worked for over four centuries, long before there was a border separating Mexico and the United States. Only after 1847, when the United States fought and won a war against Mexico, could the term "immigrant" really be used to refer to people who came from Mexico.

Beginning in the West

In fact, much of the culture and way of life in what became the American Southwest owes a debt to people who became American not by immigration but by conquest. It was, for example, the Mexican American vaqueros (cowboys) who taught the European Americans how to rope and herd livestock on the open range, and Mexican American rancheros first established the customs and practices used on vast cattle ranches of what became the southwestern states. Later, the knowledge among Mexican Americans of how to live in the harsh lands of the West helped turn those arid wastes into rich agricultural lands. Even following the influx of other immigrant groups into the American West, the Spanish names for the rivers, mountains, valleys, and settlements continued to be used, bearing witness to the impact Mexican Americans have had upon the region's culture. Yet for many years Mexican Americans' contributions were overlooked. Their offerings were invisible as they quietly went about their lives in the cities and countryside.

In the Twentieth Century

The first great wave of immigration from Mexico began with the Mexican Revolution and lasted from 1910 to 1930. About 1 million people came to the United States from Mexico during these years. Many who entered the United States dur-ing these decades thought they would go back when the fighting at home died down. But they stayed and lived out their lives in the United States because they had found the economic security they desired and increased opportunities for their children.

After World War II, a larger wave of immigrants entered the United States, some with, and others without, permission of the federal government. And since 1965, the largest wave of Mexican people has crossed the border into the United States. With the ongoing immigration from Mexico, today about 20 million Mexicans and Mexican Americans live in the United States, with Texas and California being home to more than half of them.

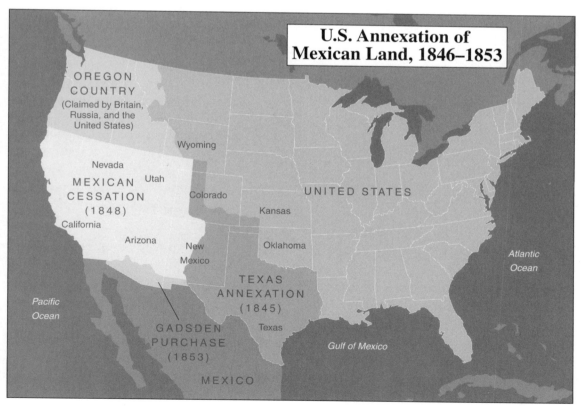

U.S. Annexation of Mexican Land, 1846–1853

OREGON COUNTRY (Claimed by Britain, Russia, and the United States)

Wyoming

Nevada

MEXICAN CESSATION (1848)

Utah

Colorado

California

Kansas

Arizona

New Mexico

Oklahoma

UNITED STATES

Atlantic Ocean

Pacific Ocean

TEXAS ANNEXATION (1845)

GADSDEN PURCHASE (1853)

Texas

Gulf of Mexico

MEXICO

An immigrant talks with a Mexican friend through a fence at the California-Mexico border. Many Mexican Americans maintain close ties with Mexico.

though most immigrant groups experience some isolation, the geographic proximity of Mexico has tended to intensify the phenomenon. Proximity has allowed Mexican Americans to keep in close contact with the land of their ancestors. Today, a Mexican American family residing in Laredo, Texas, may have relatives living just over the border in Nuevo Laredo, Mexico. This kind of binationalism exists in many border communities. People who live in one country may work, shop, travel, visit relatives, or even attend school in the other country. Because of this constant coming and going, some people say border towns have a culture all their own.

A New Culture Emerges

Mexican Americans never forgot their roots and the customs of their forebears, but until the 1960s much of their cultural contributions to the United States went unrecognized. Since the advent of the Chicano movement, however, there has been a greater appreciation of the importance of Mexican American traditions and how they have enriched American life.

Despite having lived in the United States for generations, many Mexican Americans have experienced isolation from mainstream society. In part, this isolation is the result of racial prejudice on the part of Anglo society, as well as the constant influx of new immigrants. Al-

When Mexicans came to the United States, they brought with them their love and respect for family. They also brought along a remarkable and colorful artistic tradition that has changed the American art world forever. Their vibrant musical traditions continue to echo across the land in both English and Spanish.

Even as Mexican Americans contributed to the cultural landscape of the United States, so too has the United Stated had its effect on Mexican Americans. Mexican Americans retain pride in their unique heritage even while becoming fully integrated into the American cultural mainstream. Many Mexican Americans pride themselves on their ability to speak both Spanish and English. They celebrate both traditional Mexican holidays such as Cinco de Mayo and U.S. Independence Day on the Fourth of July. This cultural interplay, then, has enhanced the whole of American society. Mexican immigrants and their descendants gave much to their new country. Keeping their dreams and traditions alive, they settled into the United States and left their indelible mark upon the land and its people.

CHAPTER ONE

Life in Mexico

In the decades following the Mexican American War, Mexico was a nation mired in seemingly unending poverty. Campesinos (peasants) found it difficult to survive as wealthy landowners increased their holdings by illegally taking water rights or by simply expropriating land. Those who did not farm but instead subsisted by mining gold and silver lived no better; they labored for a pittance while enriching the privileged few who owned the mines. In the cities, the poor worked long hours in construction or as servants for the wealthy, but had little hope for a better life.

Adding to the misery was political unrest as various political factions fought for control of the Mexican government. In this climate of political instability, repression, and poverty, many Mexicans sought to head north for the relative prosperity and peace they saw across the border in the United States.

Village Life

For most of the nineteenth century, the majority of Mexicans lived as campesinos in small rural villages. Whole families worked the land, growing corn, squash, chilies, and beans, and caring for the chickens, ducks, goats, or cows they relied on for the eggs and meat to supplement their meager diets. As poor as they were, villagers had the land they needed because they followed the *ejido* system, which allowed all families use of lands held in common for farming and for grazing their animals.

Even with communal lands to share, however, making a living in farming was chancy at best. Corn, the staple crop, grew during the rainy season from May to November, and if the weather cooperated, peasants could feed themselves all year long. But in the event of a drought or heavier-than-normal rains or an early frost, the crop could be reduced or lost altogether and the family would go hungry. When this happened, some, with starvation their only alternative, would leave their farms and go to work on the haciendas belonging to the wealthy landowners. There, at least, they would be fed.

Life in the Mines

Other peasant farmers left the land to find work in the mines, where people had extracted the mineral wealth from the earth since Mexico's early years as a Spanish colony. In the mines men labored hour after hour in the dark, digging up silver, copper, gold, lead, and tin. Even boys as young as eight or nine often worked at the mines.

One Mexican recalls the job he had with a mining company as a young boy:

They kept me busy outside the mine. A young person was not allowed to enter inside. There were only grown men inside the mines. They had about fifteen or twenty boys there, along with an old man who watched us and told us what to do. Our job was to separate the good ore from the bad. The worthless metal we piled up. . . . And the good metal we split. We always carried a hammer to break the metal into a certain size. The metal had to be small because in those times there were only a few types of machinery. The metal was taken to the smelter ready for processing because there was no rock crusher. We were the rock crusher![1]

The *Porfiriato*

After years of economic decline, Mexico had descended into a state of lawlessness. Gangs of bandits roamed freely through the countryside robbing travelers and terrorizing villagers. In 1876 Porfirio Díaz overthrew Mexico's president. Díaz promised to return order to Mexico. To those who supported his coup, Díaz gave state governorships and other political offices. Although Díaz stepped down from the presidency in the election of 1880, he remained the power behind the office. In 1880 he won election to another term as president and held on to the office for the next thirty years. This dictatorship became known as the *Porfiriato*.

In an attempt to quell peasant uprisings and bring order to the countryside, Díaz used a group known as the *Rurales* to enforce laws. Many of these men, however, were the same ruffians who were responsible for the mayhem in the first place. Not only were the *Rurales* made up of criminals, but these troops of scoundrels

Joaquin Murieta: Frontier Folk Hero

When gold was discovered in California in 1849, Mexican miners arrived to join local Mexican Americans staking their claims in gold country. Many disliked the gringos [white Americans] who came west, but some American miners believed Mexicans and Mexican Americans had no rights to the gold found on U.S. territory. So more than two thousand European American miners attacked the Sonoran mines with guns blazing and rounded up more than one hundred Mexican Americans and drove them into a corral, later hanging and killing several. The gringos set fires and burned the mining camps to the ground. The fighting lasted over a week, and many of the miners fled their claims and headed to Southern California. One of those who went south was Joaquin Murieta. He became the leader of a famous gang of banditos (bandits).

In the mid-1800s, Joaquin Murieta sought to correct the injustices of the American takeover of longtime Mexican lands after the war with the United States and the treatment of ethnic Mexican Americans in the land of their birth. Murieta gathered two thousand men to fight for justice and for the rights of those who had been deprived of their property and land.

Murieta's band of men raided herds of cattle and looted gringo rancheros and settlements, determined to bring frontier justice to California. By 1851 Joaquin Murieta had grown famous for his war against the gringos, though historians believe that other local bandits many have gotten credit for some of Murieta's raids. Still, old Californians, both Anglo and Mexican, approved of his forays.

Joaquin Murieta was a folk legend by the time he was captured by vigilantes and executed in 1853. To many Mexican Americans, he remains the heroic avenger of gringo domination and racism. Even into the twenty-first century his name reminds Mexican Americans of an early hero who had fought injustice and discrimination.

were easily bribed and had little concern for the campesinos.

As a consequence, the wealthy hacienda owners could do as they pleased, seizing peasant lands or forcing peasants to work for them. If villagers protested the treatment by hacienda owners, the *Rurales* were there to root out the leaders, put them in jail, or worse yet, simply hang them. The peasants came to fear the *Rurales* and hid when these armed bands entered their village.

Díaz Tries to Modernize Mexico

In his attempts to bring order to the country, Díaz had assumed dictatorial power.

He imposed strict controls on Mexico's previously free press and stopped all political opposition. Díaz promised to bring progress and prosperity to Mexico by modernizing the country with telegraph lines, railroads, new seaports, and factories. He also encouraged the planting of crops for the export market.

As Mexico pushed to modernize, however, life for most rural Mexicans grew even more difficult. Believing that plantations and haciendas could grow crops for export more efficiently than small farms could, Díaz looked the other way as wealthy landowners seized peasant farms and *ejido* lands. Peasants who lost their holdings had little hope of recovering them. A peasant might protest that he had the title to the land, but local officials and the courts decided the legitimacy of those claims. Mexico's elite could simply bribe judges and other officials to support their claims to the acreage they wanted. As a result of such corruption, more and more land that had been held by Mexican peasants fell into the hands of *los ricos* (the rich).

The ensuing years saw a massive concentration of wealth among a very few Mexicans and foreign investors. From 1883 to 1895, rich Mexicans as well as foreigners acquired over 70 million acres of land in the countryside. At the end of this period only 20 percent of all Mexicans still owned land. That trend continued, and by 1910 only about 2 percent of all Mexicans held any land of their own. Most of the rural populace was forced to work on the plantations and haciendas or in the mines belonging to just 834 powerful Mexican families or foreign companies.

The land seizures under the Díaz dictatorship also resulted in farmers being ever on the move in a search of jobs that would allow them to survive. Gonzalo Plancart describes how he suffered under the *Porfiriato*. Gonzalo and his father traveled northward from their native state of Guanajuato, moving from place to place, trying to make a living. Finally the only option for Gonzalo was to try his luck across the border in the United States:

> I was a motherless child and had to work very hard at farm work with my father from the time I was very small. My father worked shares [rented land] and had a number of farm animals, but [the estate owner] told him to leave. . . . We then went to Michoacán [a state farther north in Mexico] and worked for a time, but the same thing happened. We thus kept going from one place to another until my father had to sell his livestock. My father died in 1900 and then I came to the United States and worked on the railroad for two years.[2]

The Haciendas

While some peasants moved from place to place, others decided to seek work on the big estates or haciendas. Families who had previously lived independently on the *ejido* lands or who had owned their own small farms were soon held in virtual bondage on the great haciendas. Known as peons, these people were free to leave the hacienda only if they owed no money to the owner. But peons earned an average daily wage of thirty-five centavos, and with that they had to buy their beans, corn, chilies, and everything else they needed from the hacienda stores. The hacienda stores charged high prices but would extend credit, knowing full well that customers could not pay back the debt. Each year, peons grew deeper and deeper into debt until they became virtual slaves to the hacienda and its owner.

Under such a system, there was little danger of peons leaving the hacienda, and as a result, the owners felt no obligation to treat them with any dignity. In fact, most were treated more like animals than humans. Often they were forced to live in tiny huts made of cornstalks, bamboo, or adobe, with no sanitary facilities or access to clean water.

Author Jonathan Kandell, in his book *La Capital*, quotes an account by Ethel Tweedie, an Englishwoman traveling in Mexico in 1900, which describes the system of a large sugar-growing plantation in the state of Morelos, where she was a guest:

The peons' quarter [is] a veritable "village, containing nearly three thousand

Peasants look on as hacienda administrators conduct business. Hacienda workers were gernerally paid little and treated poorly by their employers.

souls, [and it] belongs to the hacienda." She [Mrs. Tweedie] accepted . . . her hosts' explanation that "the people pay no rent, and the owners of the hacienda hold the right to turn them out." But she concluded that at best "hacienda life resembles that of England in [feudal times]" and that often the debt peonage system "renders the people little more than slaves."[3]

About the same time, another Englishwoman, Rosa King, described the cruel treatment of peons:

"The manager would tighten up on the overseers, and the overseers would drive the peons, with whips if necessary," wrote Mrs. King. "I would see the poor wretches as I drove about, their feet always bare and hardened like stones, their backs bent under burdens too heavy for a horse or mule, treated as people with hearts would not treat animals."[4]

Worsening Rural Conditions

Village men who managed to retain their independence looked for seasonal work or temporary jobs in the cities to help their family survive. From southwestern states of Oaxaca and Michoacán or central states such as San Luis Potosí, Querétaro, Hidalgo, Guanajuato, and Jalisco, men looking for work migrated to Mexico City, northern Mexico, or even across the border in what had become the states and territories of Texas, Oklahoma, Arizona, New Mexico, and California.

Those who crossed the border seldom planned to stay and some returned to Mexico once they saved up enough money to support themselves and their families for a time. These returnees described the good jobs that were available and money to be made in the United States. They told how one could earn enough to live and still have money left over to bring back home to their families. Peons, too, heard these stories and concluded their only hope for a better life was to flee the hacienda and cross the border.

The Mexican Revolution

Both the lure of jobs and political freedom encouraged the first trickle of immigrants to the United States, but before long conditions at home provided an even stronger incentive to move north. By 1910 even some of Mexico's elite were fed up with Díaz and his dictatorship. They wanted to return Mexico to democratic rule. That year Francisco Madero, a wealthy man living in Mexico City, called for freedom of press, of speech, and for fair elections as provided in the Mexican constitution. But when Madero attempted to run for president, Díaz had him jailed. That move proved Díaz's undoing. Before long a cry for revolution spread across the country. In both the north and the south rebel leaders rose up vowing to end the *Porfiriato* by force.

Terror in the Countryside

Díaz's repressive rule was replaced by chaos. Government troops burned villages

Baja California Norte

Sonora

Chihuahua

Coahuila

UNITED STATES

Sinaloa

Baja California Sur

Durango

Nuevo Leon

Gulf of Mexico

Zacatecas

Tamaulipas

Nayarit

San Luis Potosì

Aguascalientes

Guanajuato

Querétaro

Hidalgo

Pacific Ocean

Jalisco

Tlaxcala

Veracruz

Yucatan

Mexico City

Campeche

Colima

Puebla

Quintana Roo

Michoacán

Tabasco

Mexico State

Federal District

Oaxaca

Chiapas

Morelos

Guerrero

and crops on the theory that doing so would stop rebel forces by depriving them of food and shelter. Various rebel factions, such as the followers of Emiliano Zapata in the state of Morelos, ran off or killed hacienda owners and reclaimed their lands for the peasants. Others, like the followers of Pancho Villa, pillaged towns whose residents remained loyal to the government; destroyed railroad lines; murdered rich shopkeepers; and even killed priests and nuns in the monasteries and convents, believing the Roman Catholic Church supported the wealthy against the peasants.

By 1911 Díaz lost control of much of the country, and the dictator barely escaped Mexico with his life. The fall of Díaz only temporarily ended the violence. Having toppled the dictator, the different rebel groups soon began fighting among themselves. As troops from different factions continued to steal, burn crops, destroy mines, or execute those whom they considered enemies of the revolution, many Mexicans caught in the middle sought refuge across the border in the United States.

The First Great Wave of Immigration to the United States

From 1910 to 1920, as a result of the violence, hunger, and general chaos during the Mexican Revolution, more than 10 percent of Mexico's population, or about 1 million people, sought safety in the United States. For some, it was merely a matter of joining relatives already living in the United States. Despite the difficulties at home, this made the decision to leave easier. They would join aunts, uncles, cousins, or sons and daughters and begin a new life. For others, such a move was a journey into the unknown, leaving everything they knew behind. Sometimes one family member crossed the border alone and later sent money so the rest of the family could come north.

Often the move north was made easier because labor recruiters, known as *enganchadores*, came from the United States looking for workers and helped finance the journey. Ernesto Galarza was just a schoolboy when his uncle Gustavo found work through a railroad labor agent. Galarza remembers,

Emiliano Zapata and the Mexican Revolution

Some say the Mexican Revolution began in a village of four hundred people, when thirty-year-old Emiliano Zapata won election as the city mayor in 1909. Zapata owned some land and cattle and had worked as a muleteer, broncobuster, and horse trainer for rich hacienda owners. Yet when village fields and water were taken over by the owner of a sugar plantation, Zapata led eighty gun-carrying villagers to reclaim their lands. When other hacienda owners tried to take over other village lands in the region, Zapata rode with campesinos to reclaim their birthright. His followers became known as Zapatistas and they set about to liberate the peasants from their downtrodden life.

Jonathan Kandell recounts in *La Capital* how upon seeing them fight for their rights, an English widow living in Mexico described Zapata's troops, saying, "the Zapatistas were not an army; they were a people in arms. [So bad was the Díaz dictatorship, it] turned the Zapatistas into fighting demons. The women cooled and reloaded the guns and scoured the country for food for the men, and old people and young children endured the hardships of their lot without complaint."

Emiliano Zapata (right) inspired many Mexican peasants to join the revolution.

Gustavo announced one night that he had talked with a labor recruiter for the Southern Pacific Railroad. The *enganchador* had told him that the railroad company was laying track . . . [and] he could find steady work and good wages. More than that the company would give him an advance in cash which could be paid back later.

It was the *enganchador* who changed the family plans. He persuaded not only Gustavo but also [uncle] José to sign up. The arrangement was that Gustavo and José would give us [my mother and me] the advance [in pay] from the Southern Pacific on which we could live temporarily. The work, the *enganchador* said, would be steady. My uncles would soon have passes on the train, so that both ourselves and Aunt Esther's family could travel north [and join all the family together again].[5]

Crossing Over

Families like Galarza's had many ways to reach the United States, but the trip was often dangerous. During the Mexican Revolution, soldiers and bands of marauders might attack would-be emigrants, taking their food, money, or anything else they thought they could use. Maria Mar-

Ernesto Galarza

Ernesto Galarza is recognized as one of the major Mexican American activists and intellectuals. Galarza wrote of his boyhood in Mexico and California in his autobiography *Barrio Boy*, and many of his own words are quoted throughout this book.

Galarza was born in 1905 in a small village in the Sierra Madre of Mexico. His family, however, emigrated to escape the Mexican Revolution in 1910, and Ernesto grew up in Sacramento, California. He attended Occidental College in Southern California in 1923 where he met only five other Mexican American students. Galarza then went on to Stanford University for graduate studies—the first Mexican American to do so. Galarza recalls how he was considered a curiosity "because white students didn't know what a Mexican looked like." While at Stanford, Galarza spoke out on behalf of immigrant workers, making him the first Mexican American student activist.

Galarza went east and earned a doctorate from Columbia University, but after graduation he took no permanent college teaching job. Instead, he devoted many years to organizing and helping agricultural workers. Working in the fields with the laborers, gathering data, testifying before government committees, or writing books on the problems facing "laborers in the fields," Galarza was a voice for those who grew America's food.

quez Zandstra explains how her family crossed the border during the dangerous years of the Mexican Revolution:

We were traveling on a train. I believe it was from Zacatecas [a city in northern Mexico] to the north. It was night and very, very dark. We were supposed to be very quiet; they were trying to sneak the train through enemy lines. The seats lined the sides [of the train car]. . . . It was dark and my feet dangled. I remember looking down at my shoes, which had little buttons. I distinctly remember that, and being scared, then the lights, tiny lights in the distance. That is my first recollection. . . . After that I don't recall anything until we came to El Paso.[6]

Even if there were no rebel or government troops in the region, the crossing could be difficult. Some families, lacking the money to take a train, packed their few belongings on mules or horses or in wagons and set out across the rugged arid lands of northern Mexico. Upon reaching the border, they continued into California, New Mexico, Texas, or Arizona. These families faced all manner of difficulties along the trail—walking or riding through desert, crossing mountains, facing scorching sun or occasionally pelting rains.

Others, if circumstances permitted, simply made the crossing at one of the established border towns. Luis Murillo, who had ridden with Pancho Villa during the Mexican Revolution, was one who just walked across the border. Eventually, he moved to Laredo, Mexico, a city across the Rio Grande from Laredo, Texas. Murillo explains: "I kept my taste for adventure from being a soldier so much and on the 2 of August 1920 I crossed the bridge to this [the U.S.] side of Laredo. As I had been living for some time in Laredo [Mexico] it only cost me a nickel toll. I worked on the farms on this side."[7]

By the 1920s, hundreds of thousands of Mexican immigrants had entered the United States through border towns like San Diego or Calexico, California, and El Paso, Brownsville, or Laredo, Texas.

The great wave of immigration that began during the Mexican Revolution lasted until the 1930s. Whatever their circumstances and however they entered the United States, these immigrants all held high hopes of finding work and a better life.

CHAPTER TWO

Working in *el Norte* (the North)

The combination of political unrest and harsh economic conditions at home swelled Mexican immigration. Still, life for the immigrants once they arrived in the United States was anything but easy. Those Mexicans who came in the late nineteenth and early twentieth centuries arrived with almost nothing in the way of money or resources. For those lucky enough to have experience building railroads or working in mines, there were jobs available. Most, however, had been peons or peasant farmers. Lacking skills, they had to take what jobs they could find. Whatever they did, most worked hard, hoping to prosper in the land of opportunity.

Building the Railroads

In the early years of the twentieth century, *enganchadores* contracted with immigrants for jobs on the railroads or for large commercial farms in Texas, Oklahoma, Colorado, or California. These labor recruiters, both American and Mexican, collected groups of men at the border, promising good wages, and then transported workers and their families to commercial farms or railroad camps. Those recruited for the railroad went to lay track in the West or to cities like Los Angeles or Chicago, where they built train and trolley lines.

The railroads had been trying to lure Mexican workers to the United States since about 1900, and the Mexican Revolution proved a boon to these companies. In one month during 1910, for example, more than two thousand Mexican immigrants crossed the border into El Paso to head to railroad camps. Those immigrants took jobs laying track as far north as Colorado, Wyoming, Utah, Montana, Oregon, Washington, and Idaho. In Southern California alone, the Southern Pacific and Santa Fe railroads brought in two to three carloads of immigrants a week to work building lines serving the growing cities of Los Angeles and San Diego.

Building and maintaining railroads was backbreaking work performed under difficult conditions. After leveling or grading the ground, workers hauled heavy iron rails over the wooden crossties and then drove in thick spikes to fasten down the rails. Much of the land where they laid or repaired the tracks was flat dry plains or desert, and temperatures during summer days often reached over one hundred degrees. During the brief springtime, torrential rains might suddenly flood low areas and wash out tracks. In the mountain passes during the winter, snows fell and sometimes piled up as high as a man's waist, making it difficult to move. The willingness of the immigrants to take on such demanding jobs earned them admiration

Working on the Railroad and Living in a Boxcar

Although the immigrants' labor was vital in the effort to build and repair railroads, their employers showed little concern for providing adequate living accommodations for their workers. While building or repairing railroad lines or railcars, the immigrant families lived in labor camps, separated from the local townspeople. Sometimes these camps were no more than old boxcars.

In the book *Mexican-Origin People in the United States* by Oscar J. Martinez, historian Michael Smith describes such a camp as it existed in Kansas City in the 1910s:

Most railroad workers typically lived in boxcar camps. In these crude settlements, situated in the [railroad] yards or on the sidings, workers slept on straw or rough bunks. Even the "improved" housing, which the Santa Fe [railroad] furnished for its workers after 1912, consisted of uncomfortable shacks made from scrap pieces and cheap secondhand materials including old tires, rails, and sheet metal. The company supplied no furniture, plumbing, or electrical facilities. Workers assigned to the yards often lived packed together in a single large building called a section house; others crammed into small two-room sections huts.

from Anglos. Historian Oscar J. Martinez quotes two men who observed Mexican laborers at work:

"You see that poor devil out there lifting that heavy iron? He is as strong as an ox. . . . Right now he has to have two pairs of gloves so as not to blister his calloused hands. Those are Mexicans. . . . They work when we are sleeping, mush around in the water in big rains. . . . When a wreck occurs, they are the first to get there though it be, as it usually is at night . . . ."

"Yes, [the other replied]. . . . They are doing work that the average American would not and cannot think of doing. Last week . . . in the desert the heat killed three Mexicans and prostrated [laid flat] a score [as twenty] more. The temperature was up to 120 degrees."[8]

Others were less charitable in their view of immigrants, suggesting that such tasks were all the Mexicans deserved. The U.S. commissioner-general of immigration stated his racist views that Mexicans were naturally suited to railroad work: "The peon makes a satisfactory track hand for the reasons that he is docile, ignorant, and nonclannish to an extent which makes it possible that one or more men shall quit or be discharged and others remain at work; moreover, he is willing to work for a low wage."[9]

A few immigrants found jobs in the rail shops repairing equipment or building railroad cars. Such work was much easier than laying track or repairing the thousands of miles of rail lines running throughout the West.

The Mining Industry in the United States

Like their countrymen who found work building or maintaining the railroads, Mexican immigrants who had worked in the mines at home readily found jobs in the United States. Still, these jobs were hard, dirty, and above all, dangerous. Miners descended deep into the earth for long hours to dig out the ores and minerals. In winter when days were short, some miners rarely saw the sun, as they went into the mines before sunrise and came out only to see the dark night sky. As historian Richard E. Lingenfelter explains,

The miner usually worked a shift of from eight to ten hours. . . . Beginning his day, he . . . was lowered down the shaft. In a large mine he might descend at 400 feet a minute. . . . When he reached the level where he was to work, he picked up his candles, drills, hammer, pick or shovel at the station and went to the spot assigned him. The candles were either attached to his cap or mounted in steel holders that could be driven into a crack in the rock. In some mines the miner was rationed to three candles per ten-hour shift and if he used them too fast he had grope through the last of his shift in darkness.[10]

Once in America, Mexican immigrants went to work at a variety of jobs. Many became miners like these men.

Working deep in the mines was perilous. As miners attacked the rock with picks and drills, mineshafts might collapse, burying the men alive. Sometimes miners would not be buried under debris but be trapped after a cave-in blocked their escape. Even for the miners who escaped immediate death from cave-ins, the danger from poisonous or explosive gas was often present.

Despite the risks, miners arrived from the Mexican states of Baja California, Sonora, Chihuahua, and other states. They went to work in the copper, gold, and silver mines throughout the West, and in coal mines in Oklahoma and New Mexico. Yet employers kept the skilled jobs for the American miners and gave Mexican immigrants the worst jobs. Besides favoritism by management, Mexican miners faced hostility from Anglo miners who, despite their advantaged positions, viewed the immigrants as a threat to their own jobs.

Immigrant Labor Builds Agriculture in the Southwest

While some immigrants found work in the railroads and the mines, many others took jobs in agriculture. Landowners in arid

Rudy and the Short Hoe

Up until the second half of the twentieth century, migrant farmworkers had been forced to use a short hoe for getting close to the soil. This tool had a flat blade attached to one end. Because of the short handle, many migrants experienced terrible back pain from stooping for hours in the fields. Eventually the short hoes were outlawed. But the migrant Treviño family found a good use for one as Elva Treviño Hart tells in her autobiography, *Barefoot Heart.* Although her father knew the law banned young children from laboring in the fields, her ten-year-old brother begged to do grown-up work, and so her father finally relented:

> The short hoe was perfect for Rudy, since he had just finished the fourth grade and was only four feet tall.

He insisted on working, so my father devised a way for him to do it. The family put stakes at the ends of the rows they planned to work labeled 'L. Trevino.' Usually, my father worked two rows at a time. . . . Everyone else took one row. But they didn't start right at the edge of the field; they started thirty feet in. Rudy, with his short hoe, worked the first thirty feet of everyone's row. But he was to keep one eye out for gringos. If any drove up or drove by, he was to drop his short hoe and walk away nonchalantly, or pretend to be playing. We didn't know what would happen if my father got caught violating the child labor laws.

states like Texas, Oklahoma, Colorado, and California benefited from the knowledge of Mexicans who had long known the techniques needed to help crops flourish and grow in dry conditions. The ready supply of Mexican labor, along with the network of rail lines to move produce, made commercial farming possible.

Acre after acre of ground was prepared by hand by Mexican immigrants. First they cleared the land of the brush, cactus, chaparral, and an occasional tree. The immigrants "grubbed" out most of the brush using short hoes. Then they leveled the fields, breaking up the dirt clods and clearing away the rocks they found. To bring in the water crops would need, thousands of immigrants labored digging irrigation ditches. Their labor literally made the dry lands bloom.

Stooping in the fields, farmworkers planted, pruned, weeded, and harvested the crops—sugar beets, cotton, oranges, lemons, grapes, grapefruit, pecans, tomatoes, lettuce, and more. Often, the whole family, even the children, worked in the fields. Ventura Gomez was a mother of four children living with her family in Iowa when she told about her experiences picking cotton: "When I was little, picking cotton, I didn't have a sack [to put the cotton in]. I would go in front of my mama and leave little piles for her. When I was older I had my own sack. . . . It made me very happy, because I was very little and the money I earned was mine."[11]

Once harvested, the crops needed to be packed or canned or otherwise processed. Mexican immigrants, mostly women, provided most of the labor in many of the processing plants and canneries. They stood inside sweltering sheds on the edge of the fields or orchards washing, cutting, or cooking the peaches, pears, apricots, tomatoes, or other fruits and vegetables and putting them in the cans and jars.

Ranch Hands

In the same way Mexican immigrants found jobs in agriculture in the Southwest, so, too, did their knowledge help them get work as ranch hands on the cattle and sheep ranches of California, New Mexico, Colorado, Arizona, and Texas. Immigrants and Mexican American vaqueros (cowboys) rode their horses on the open range, keeping watch on the cattle that were raised for their hides and meat.

Mexican American and immigrant shepherds and sheepshearers applied their skills to the large sheep ranches. The shepherds watched over the flocks grazing on the open lands, and the sheepshearers worked every spring traveling from place to place throughout the West to clip the wool. Sheepshearers were usually paid a certain amount for each sheep they sheared, and for some it was seasonal work only. Other immigrants labored year-round on the sheep ranches.

Getting "Mexican Wages"

Although Mexican immigrants had little trouble finding employment in the United

Vaqueros and Cowboys on the Frontier

Many of the practices adopted in the nineteenth century by Anglo cowboys had long been used by Mexican vaqueros, who herded cattle on the rancheros of Mexico, California, and Texas. For example, the saddle the Anglo cowboys strapped on their horses came from the horned saddle used by the vaqueros. The Mexican Americans took the soft wood of the giant prickly pear cactus and made a flat saddle with a horn. The horns anchored the steers they lassoed (from the Spanish word *lazo*).

Each year when the new calves were born, the ranch's own branding iron was used to burn its symbol or brand on its cattle, and of course, American ranchers and cowboys adopted this custom. Modern-day cowboys or ranch hands still hold rodeos, using the techniques developed by the old vaqueros as they rounded up their cattle for branding.

States during the early years of the twentieth century, they worked in the poorest conditions and received less pay than other workers did for the same jobs. On the railroads, they were treated worse than other railroad employees and paid according to a different scale. The Japanese railroad workers, for example, received $1.45 a day and the Greeks got $1.60, but those of Mexican descent were paid only $1.25 a day. As a result, Mexican immigrants moved on as they found better opportunities, and many who had started with the railroads later became field hands or miners.

Just as in railroad work, Mexican American immigrant miners received less pay than other workers. Most mining companies had a special payroll grade—"Mexican labor," which meant less pay than others immigrants. From 1895 to 1910, the average wage for unskilled workers of Mexican origin stood at about $2 per day. But the wage paid to unskilled laborers of European descent was about $4 per day. This two-tiered system in the mines remained in effect until the 1940s. Nonetheless, from 1900 to 1940, Mexican immigrants provided 60 percent of the unskilled labor in the mines of the Southwest.

Mexican immigrant women, too, earned less than other immigrant women. Besides cannery and fieldwork, Mexican American women often held jobs as domestic help, cooks, dishwashers, seamstresses, or laundry workers. But whatever they did, they received less pay than other immigrant women did for the same work. In El Paso laundries, for example, Women of Mexican descent got only $6 per week, while Anglo workers received $17.

Early Labor Unions

Immigrants struggled against the obvious discrimination they experienced. Sometimes labor unions such as the American Federation of Labor (AFL) or the International Workers of the World (IWW) would allow these immigrants to join, but other unions, such as the Western Federation of Miners (WFM), discriminated against them. In such cases, or if no union existed, the immigrants formed their own unions to help improve working conditions.

Even before the large influx of Mexican immigrants arrived, between 1901 and 1903, in rural areas around San Francisco, Fresno, Redlands, and San Diego, California, Mexican immigrant workers went on strike demanding fair pay and better working conditions. In Santa Barbara, California, fruit packers walked off the job, calling for shorter hours and adequate pay. Mexican American railroad workers in the Unión Federal Mexicana went on strike against the Pacific Electric streetcar lines. Immigrant miners across the West stopped work, protesting dangerous conditions in the mines and the unequal pay system.

In the first several decades of the twentieth century, these efforts brought mixed results. In 1913, for example, in the Sacramento Valley of California at the Durst Ranch, IWW workers left the fields, demanding a fair wage, separate toilet facilities for men and women, and drinking water in the fields at least twice a day. Management called in National Guard troops who forced the strikers back to the fields without an agreement regarding their demands.

The Miners of the Clifton-Morenci Strike

Miners of Mexican descent in the Southwest had a long history of taking precious metals from the earth. Yet Mexican American miners faced discrimination in the mines in the Southwest. The unfair treatment, especially in the copper mines of Arizona, included segregating the workers and their families into Mexican camps. Besides separate housing, the two-tiered pay scales gave Mexican Americans less money for the same jobs, and racial discrimination excluded them from the Western Federation of Miners (WFM) union.

The WFM hoped to drive Mexican Americans and immigrants from the Arizona mines, but Mexican American miners remained determined to improve their conditions. Without being allowed to join Anglo unions, they found labor cooperation difficult. Still, they devised a way to get a work stoppage at the mines in Clifton-Morenci in 1903.

The Arizona legislature, encouraged by the WFM, passed a bill prohibiting miners from working more than eight hours instead of the previous ten. The mine owners followed the law, but cut workers' salaries to match the new hours. With already lower wages, this meant Mexican Americans could not survive with the cut in pay. They walked out in protest, demonstrated in town, and so stopped the mines from operating for several days. No one had suspected that Mexican Americans had the power to halt production.

Soon, however, the Arizona Rangers, federal troops, and the National Guard arrived to force these striking miners back on the job, and when sudden heavy rains brought flooding, the strike ended. Many of the leaders were arrested, jailed, and then deported to Mexico.

The discriminatory practices and wages continued in the mines at Clifton-Morenci, but many of the original strikers moved on to other mines in other states.

Some triumphs, though, came during the 1930s when a union of agricultural workers known as CUCOM, for Confederación de Uniones de Campesinos y Obreros Mexicanos, arose. The union represented about ten thousand workers. In California CUCOM led successful strikes in orange orchards, packing plants, and on celery farms. In 1937 this union joined the United Cannery, Agricultural, Packing, and Allied Workers of America, UCAPAWA, and after a three-month strike against unfair wages and difficult working conditions, UCAPAWA obtained improvements and gained influence in the cannery industry.

Again and again in the first part of the twentieth century, Mexican immigrants struggled to improve their lot by asking for living wages, limits on work hours, safe working conditions, and rules barring discrimination based on ethnicity. Yet even though some workers succeeded in having such demands met, large growers usually won out by bringing in strikebreakers, having striking workers arrested for disturbing the peace or trespassing, or by placing inflammatory reports in local newspapers to turn public opinion against labor organizers.

Migrant Laborers

The immigrants' problems during the early 1930s became even more acute by the worldwide economic downturn known as the Great Depression. Adding to the difficulties was a lengthy drought that resulted in small crop yields for farmers of the Southwest. Some early immigrants who had managed to acquire small farms of their own lost their land when the crop failures left them unable to pay their taxes or mortgages. Left homeless, these former landowners were forced to migrate from place to place, seeking work in the fields, bringing in whatever crops were ready to harvest.

Even though the Great Depression had largely ended by the 1940s, hard times lingered for those Mexican immigrants who made their living on the farms. They

Mexican migrant workers pose in a field. The Great Depression of the 1930s forced many Mexican immigrants to become migrant farmers.

continued to travel from place to place, planting, picking, and packing the bounty of America's farmlands, struggling to earn enough money to live on. Families would pack blankets, clothes, and pots and pans into their own cars or trucks or onto buses provided by labor contractors.

Children often toiled in the orchards and fields alongside their parents. The job of planting and picking involved long hard hours in the fields, with no assurance the family would earn enough money to keep themselves housed, clothed, and fed. Typical of the migrants' experience was that of Elva Treviño Hart, the youngest child born to a Mexican American migrant family in Texas. She recalls how each spring they packed up their car and headed for farms in the Midwest. She spent her summers in the fields with her parents, two brothers, and two sisters. Their first stop each year was the same sugar beet farm in Minnesota. They lived in housing provided by the farm owner, and the whole family went off to the fields each day to work beside other migrant families. Treviño Hart describes their life on the so-called circuit:

Sometimes on Saturdays, we worked only until lunch. Then the people went back to the camp, took a bath and went grocery shopping or to do laundry. Sunday was a workday like the rest. Our getting up time was the same everyday—before dawn.

. . . After beet thinning season in Minnesota, Wisconsin was next every year. . . . In Wisconsin, the work was

sporadic and unpredictable. Sometimes we would work many days at a stretch, sometimes there were no fields that were ready to pick. On these days, we did the laundry or went swimming or fishing.

. . . In Wisconsin we always went to different farms. We never knew from one day to the next from one year to the next, where we would go or live or what we would do. The word about what kind of work was available and where came by word of mouth and by chance. This was distressing for my father because he would have liked consistent work everyday [to earn enough money], and great for the kids because they worked less.[12]

Working in Urban Environments

Increasing numbers of Mexican immigrants, meanwhile, had settled in America's growing cities. Their experience differed because they found work in a wide variety of expanding trades such as construction, cleaning and repair, public works projects, and hotels and restaurants. Mexican Americans and immigrants sought work in industries such as metals and machinery, paper, chemicals, paints, wood manufacturing, and in stone, clay, and glass products. Some jobs were located in the Southwest, but many were in the North. In pursuit of work, immigrants gradually moved out of the borderlands— the states bordering Mexico—settling in a variety of locations.

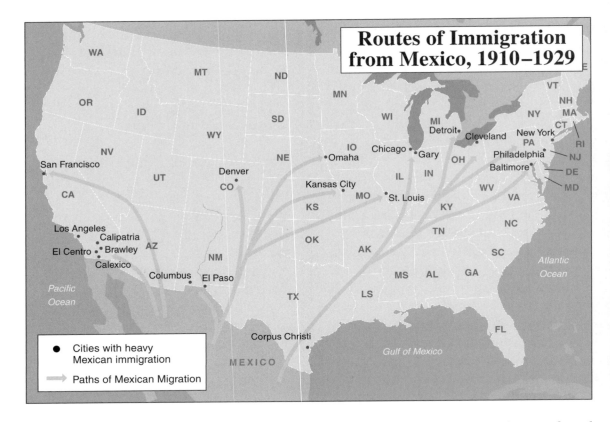

Routes of Immigration from Mexico, 1910–1929

- ● Cities with heavy Mexican immigration
- ⇒ Paths of Mexican Migration

One event that resulted in expanded opportunities for Mexican immigrants was America's entry into World War I in 1917. Large numbers of working-age men joined the armed services, opening jobs in the industrialized East and Midwest. Immigrants soon moved to fill these vacancies. This trend continued, and by the beginning of World War II, over fifty-eight thousand Mexican immigrants had traveled to Kansas, Michigan, Wisconsin, Illinois, Pennsylvania, and to other northern locations seeking jobs. They found work in the auto factories, steel mills, meatpacking plants, lumber mills, oil refineries, textile mills, farming and construction equipment factories, and on the docks in the ports of the Great Lakes.

In the Midwest most immigrants found less discrimination against Mexicans than they had found in the borderlands, and many became part of the new working class. As one immigrant who went to Chicago to find work said, "We like it here better than Texas. Wages are better . . . and there is no distinction [between the races]." Another man who worked in both the auto and steel industry agreed saying, "Distinction [or racial discrimination]? Yes, in Texas. . . . In Flint, Michigan, no. . . . I go every place . . . that's why I was living good and liked it in Pittsburgh [Pennsylvania]."[13]

Women, too, found work in the cities. In Detroit, for example, they held jobs such as janitors, maids, cigar makers, hairdressers, glass cutters, or seamstresses. Some women opened up *casas de asistencia* (boardinghouses) to help their family earn enough to get by. Historian Zaragosa Vargas describes the difficult job of running a boardinghouse:

> Operating a casa de asistencia was hard work . . . often as exhausting as the labor men performed in the factories. In addition to family duties like child rearing, women likely kept up a hectic pace all day as they fed the men coming and going on the different shifts. They had [different] cook schedules, as some men wanted breakfast at dinnertime while others wanted their dinner in the morning. Long hours were spent not only cooking and shopping for food but doing laundry and performing additional housekeeping tasks.[14]

As the first wave of immigrants took root on American soil, most had grasped a small piece of the American dream of steady work. They found the political stability they sought and hoped that prosperity could come if they continued to work hard. By the end of the Great Depression Mexican immigrants had spread to the urban centers across the country. By then they had established communities where their families could grow and flourish.

CHAPTER THREE

Communities in Transition

In their new country, people of Mexican heritage sought a place in the United States, even as they retained their cultural identity as Mexicans. With varying degrees of success, they attempted to be Mexican Americans. Even as they tried to make a place in Anglo society, Mexican Americans found their efforts hampered by the attitudes of many of their fellow citizens. For example, one Mexican American man told journalist Manuel Ruiz Ibáñez,

A man born in Germany, Ireland, England or any other European country comes to the United States and is immediately recognized as American after being naturalized [made a citizen]. Yet we are not considered as just plain Americans, despite the fact that we were born here and in many cases come from families, which have lived here for several generations. Many of us are descendants of men and women who were here way before any Anglos ever set foot on this land but still we are designated as "Mexicans."[15]

Long-Held Prejudices

Americans of Northern European descent had long focused on the differences between their culture and that of the Mexican Americans. In 1879, for example, in *The Harper's New Monthly Magazine*, a journalist contrasted Mexican Americans and Anglos in Texas in unflattering terms, saying, "These greasers are not inclined to assimilate their customs and modes to those of whites."[16] And the *New York Tribune* printed a description of San Antonio, Texas, by E.V. Smally that expressed similar attitudes:

It is a city of the most striking contrasts. Here our pushing Western civilization comes in contact with the sleepy, dead alive, half civilization of Mexico. . . . The New York drummer [salesman], arrayed in faultless garments from the Broadway shops [of New York City], jostles in narrow streets [with] the *ranchero* in *poncho* and *sombrero* and the Boston tourist . . . encounters the blanketed Indian of the plains. Here . . . modern [Protestant] churches, with carpeted aisles and cushioned pews stand in sight of a venerable Spanish cathedral where swarthy penitents, muffled in shawls crouch on the stone floor and tell their beads [pray their rosary].[17]

As a result of Anglo prejudice, most Mexican Americans lived in segregated Hispanic communities like this New Mexico town.

As a result of such attitudes among Anglos, most Mexican Americans found their opportunities restricted. With the exception of a few people of Mexican heritage who long ago had gained wealth and had intermarried with Anglos or who had allied themselves with other wealthy Americans, most Mexican Americans were systematically segregated in society. Their choice of jobs was restricted and most lived in segregated city neighborhoods— known as barrios or *colonias*—or in isolated rural communities.

Confined to the margins of society, Mexican Americans adapted in different ways. Those who had the least contact with Anglos often looked to Mexico as their cultural home; they lived in adobe houses, spoke only Spanish, told their children Mexican folktales, and kept as many of their traditions as they could. Others preserved much of their heritage but adopted Anglo modes of dress, celebrated the holidays observed by Anglos, and spoke both English and Spanish. A few, especially those who had managed to acquire wealth, were completely assimilated, though they retained their Spanish surnames.

Nativism and the Great Depression Deportations

Although Mexican Americans found ways of dealing with the prejudice they faced, in the early 1930s a general intolerance of immigrants, known as nativism, took hold in the United States. Such attitudes were not new, but in the hard times of the Great Depression sentiments against Mexican Americans in particular grew so strong that

Anglo politicians responded with programs that even included forcing Mexican Americans to move to Mexico. Many of those who were affected by such policies had lost their farms or their jobs because of the depression just as other Americans had, but Mexican Americans and immigrants, instead of being seen as victims, were blamed for the problems. In some places local officials rounded up Mexican Americans and forced them onto buses, trucks, or trains and escorted them across the border.

Repatriation policies were so unevenly and arbitrarily applied that many families were split apart. One man who was repatriated to Mexico but later returned, describes the train ride he experienced:

At the station in Santa Ana [California], hundreds of Mexicans [and Mexican Americans] came and there was quite a lot of crying.

When they arrived at Los Angeles, the repatriates were calmed a bit . . . from Los Angeles to El Paso, some sang with guitars trying to forget their sadness and others cried.

The train did not arrive at the station in El Paso but rather at the border. There was a terrible cry . . . many did not want to cross the border because many had daughters and sons who had stayed . . . married to others here [in the United States] who did not want to return to Mexico. A disaster because the majority of the families were separated. There was no way for anyone to try to leave the train or complete their desire to return to the United States.[18]

In all it is estimated that between a half million and a million Mexican Americans left the United States during the years of the Great Depression. Some later returned. The sense of betrayal felt by the Mexican American community, though, created even greater cultural isolation.

Moving to the Cities

As a result of nativism, Mexican Americans who remained in the United States increasingly found themselves even more rigorously segregated into the barrios. Not only did Mexican Americans move to the barrios when they were forced off the land by hard times, but those already living in the barrios encountered opposition if they tried to live elsewhere. In some places laws mandated separate housing sections, but just as effective were attitudes among real estate agents and developers who refused to rent or sell to Mexican Americans.

Many of the barrios were outside the local city limits and so had no public services. Even for barrios inside the city limits, municipalities usually refused to

Mexican Americans continued to preserve their cultural traditions in the barrios. Here, a couple in the Los Angeles barrio weaves straw.

provide basic services. Under such conditions, malnutrition and diseases, especially dysentery, hepatitis, and tuberculosis, were common. During the 1970s anthropologist Shirley Anchor interviewed residents who had lived all their lives in their West Dallas barrio. Describing the depression years, one of the residents told her, "It was hard in those days—really hard. People were always sick and no one had a full stomach."[19]

Such policies resulted in the creation of communities that would retain their distinctive character long after legal segregation had been outlawed. For example Anchor, writing in 1972, describes the West Dallas barrio:

> The towering downtown Dallas skyline across the river is clearly visible from any street in La Bajura [the barrio], but here is, nonetheless, a village-like quality about the neighborhood which belies its urban setting. Leafy trees shade several streets. Many residents grow flowers and greenery in their small yards, or decorate front porches with plants in colorful Mexican pots or over-sized tin cans. Some houses have small vegetable gardens in the back. Chickens are common, and the crowing of roosters is a familiar early morning sound.[20]

Life in the Barrios, *Colonias*, and Towns

Even though many Mexican Americans lived in barrios or *colonias* because they had no choice, they were places that helped preserve their cultural traditions. The language spoken was Spanish; the shop owners sold traditional foods like chilies, *pan dulce* (sweetened bread), and corn flour; Spanish language newspapers flourished; and at times young men played guitars and sang traditional Mexican folk music or radios blared *rancheras*, Mexican cowboy songs. Each year people gathered to celebrate various saints' days, especially the one for la Virgen de Guadalupe—Our Lady of Guadalupe, the patroness saint of Mexico—or to hold fiestas for Cinco de Mayo (a national Mexican holiday) or Mexican Independence on September sixteenth.

Even barrio residents born in the United States celebrated traditional Mexican holidays, keeping their cultural heritage alive in the process. Elva Treviño Hart remembers how, as a little girl in Pearsall, Texas, she waited anxiously for the Cinco de Mayo celebration. From her house she watched as people set up for the traditional celebration:

> When the band started playing, I ran over. . . . I found my friend Manuela and her two older sisters and we started the paseo. This meant walking in a circle around the platform on the thirty-foot-wide walkway. For the teenagers, this meant the girls walked in one direction and the boys in the other. Twice in every circle, they would meet each other and smile—or not smile and look the other way on purpose. This is the way initial courtship was done in Mexico at the central plaza of the town. But in

Pearsall we had no plaza, only the fiesta twice a year.[21]

Many other cultural practices continued beyond the first generation immigrants. Perhaps because of their isolation from Anglo society or because new immigrants from Mexico continued to arrive, many traditions survived in the new country. Most immigrants, for example, continued to rely on the services of a *curandero* (folk healer) as they had in Mexico. There were many kinds of *curanderos*. Some offered herbs and brews for ailments while other used objects such as raw eggs, bird feathers, or elaborate rituals to heal the sick. Some families tried the services of the *curandero* first and later went to a licensed medical doctor if the folk healer's treatment failed to bring results.

In the barrio, the tradition of family members, close friends, or godparents relying on one another—known as *compadrazgo*—remained strong. *Padrinos*, godparents, who might not be related by blood, helped out in difficult times, feeding godchildren, taking care of them if the parents were sick, even raising them as their own. Because of *compadrazgo*, Mexican American children could count several additional aunts, uncles, older brothers and sisters, grandparents, and godparents as part of their family.

In these large groups everyone had to do their part, and older children helped younger children learn their tasks. Patricia Luna recalls how the whole family assisted with the children, taking them to school, telling them stories, and teaching them to ride horseback or weed the garden. Patricia lived with her extended family on her grandfather's farm and remembers how even as a young girl she was expected to work alongside her young uncles. "My grandfather, always spoke to me as a strong person, capable of doing just about anything. . . . [I] used to do everything they [my uncles] did, work in the fields, whatever. If there was something I didn't know how to do they wouldn't do it for me, they'd teach me."[22]

Most Mexican Americans remained Roman Catholic and practiced their faith in traditional Mexican ways. For example, often in barrio parishes between December 16 and December 24 candlelight processions of children and adults—known as posadas—portrayed the journey of Mary and Joseph as they went from inn to inn searching for a place to stay. *Pastorelas* (religious plays), too, were common, dramatizing the pilgrimage of the shepherds seeking the baby Jesus.

Their Roman Catholic faith was central to many Mexican Americans' cultural identity. Frances Esquibel Tywoniak, who was born in New Mexico and is the daughter of an immigrant father and Mexican American mother recalls,

Religion, of course, was very much a part of life in rural New Mexico. My mother's family was very devoutly Roman Catholic. Catholicism defined us as much as our surname defined us. There was the church and there were the saints. . . . San Ysidero [in statue form] was carried in a religious procession through . . . the fields [and] he was asked to bless as

Curanderos

A *curandero* is a healer, but there are many kinds of healers. Some just offer *remedios* (remedies), such as *manzanilla* tea for upset stomachs or *yerba buena* tea for feeling tired or weak. In her autobiography, *Barefoot Heart*, Elva Treviño Hart recalls the *curanderos* in her town:

> There were several kinds of curanderos in Pearsall [Texas], some of whom my mother trusted implicitly, much more than a doctor, and others whom she trusted not at all. . . . There was El Cieguito [the Blind Man], who saw with his fingers. He could be trusted with any ailment of the bones or muscles. He could massage dislocations and sprains away, or else tell you when he couldn't. Then there was Doña Tacha, who worked with prayer and herbs. She could be trusted. Then there was the kind of curandero that worked with owl feathers and wild rabbit livers in the light of the new moon. Amá [my mother] would never go near this kind of curandero. But Nina [my aunt] did.

the patron saint of *los labradores*, the tillers of the soil. Santa Rita was a beautiful lady and the saint who healed wounds. Religious pictures and statues [in homes and churches] were visually appealing.[23]

In larger communities, where there was often more than one Catholic church, Mexican Americans usually attended the one located in the barrio. There, church rituals were performed as they had been in Mexico. Frances Esquibel Tywoniak, who later moved from New Mexico to Visalia, California, remembers:

> There was the regular, big Catholic Church that all Catholics in town presumably attended, but I was also aware of religious practices and customs unique to the people of the barrio.
>
> . . . I also remember one occasion where a religious procession of some kind was organized in the barrio. . . . The young boys were dressed in white trousers and white shirts with kerchiefs at their necks. They wore straw hats and carried . . . [m]iniature Mexican-style crates [that], probably contained religious images or icons.[24]

Getting an Education

If many Mexican Americans sought to retain some of their traditions, they also aspired for their children to have the option of learning the basics for success in Anglo society. Most families believed education was the key to that success. Parents often sacrificed to be sure their children got an education, and most wanted their children to get what they did not have—a high school education.

Immigrant Ernesto Galarza explains how after his mother and uncle died during an epidemic, his young uncle José took over the responsibility for him and his education. Galarza explains,

> José had chosen our new home in the basement of [the house on] O Street because it was close to the Hearkness Junior High School. As the *jefe de familia* (head of the family) he explained that I could help earn our living but that I was to study for a high school diploma. That being settled, my routine was clearly divided into schooltime and worktime, the second depending on when I was free from the first.[25]

Ernesto Galarza's experience, however, differed from that of most Mexican American students because he attended an integrated public school, whereas most Mexican immigrant children attended segregated schools. Local educators justified this practice by claiming Mexican American children needed special help because they could not speak proper English. Such arguments were undermined by even second- and third-generation Mexican Americans who were forced to attend segregated schools or separate classes just for "Mexicans." Moreover, many were encouraged to take subjects preparing them for menial employment rather than academic subjects preparing them for college.

Some parents trusted only Catholic schools, usually located in the barrio, with their children's education. In these schools immigrant children received intensive instruction aimed at helping them succeed in the Anglo world. Journalist and scholar Richard Rodriguez, for example, remembers how he, like most

Lemon Grove Demands Equal Education

In Lemon Grove, California, in 1931 when the school board built a separate two-room schoolhouse for the local Mexican American children, the immigrant community organized a "neighbors' committee" to fight the segregation. Every family but one refused to send their children to the *caballeriza* (stable), as they called it. They sought legal help and publicity and filed a suit with the Superior Court of San Diego accusing the school board of segregation.

In March 1931 the case was heard. Several school children, speaking in perfect English, took the stand to explain their desire to get a good education. The court ruled in favor of the parents and children. This was the first successful school desegregation case in the United States. Others followed, but as late as the 1980s court cases were still being filed to gain equal education for Mexican American children.

children of immigrants, began school speaking only Spanish. But,

> My earliest (first grade) teachers, the nuns, made my success their ambition. [They] went to my house one Saturday [and] . . . asked my [Spanish-speaking] parents to try to speak English at home, and so my parents did all they could to speak English and encourage us to use it. In school, meanwhile, like my brother and sister, I was required to attend a daily tutoring session. I needed a full year of special attention [to learn correct English].[26]

Although immigrant children often struggled with English, many school administrators and teachers felt the best way for students to learn the language was to use it all the time. Schools had policies under which students were punished for using Spanish even outside of class. Dionicio Morales attended public school in Southern California. He recalls what happened to him when he spoke Spanish at recess:

> Every time I was caught speaking Spanish, I would be taken to the principal's office. She would then wash my mouth out with soap at an old rusty, tin bathtub. The bitter taste of soap and water, shoved into my mouth by the teacher while she held my head down, made me feel as if I were drowning. . . . I started getting my mouth washed out when I was only six years old.[27]

Assimilation Difficulties

Punishment for speaking Spanish reflected the fact that one of the objectives of the schools serving the barrios was to promote American values and instruct Mexican American children in Anglo cultural traditions. Their teachers read them stories of George Washington, they heard about Abraham Lincoln, and teachers taught them America stood for liberty and justice for all. Yet what they experienced in real life was often at odds with what they were taught in school. Not only were Mexican Americans forced to live in barrios, but also they found movie theaters, restaurants, drugstores, or motels were entirely off-limits or, as with public swimming pools, available only on a particular day when no Anglos would be there. Signs saying "No Mexican Trade Wanted" or "No Mexicans Allowed" hung in shop windows.

Cesar Chavez, who would one day be a leading voice against the mistreatment of Mexican American laborers, recalled once when he visited a restaurant and ordered a hamburger:

> We went this one time to a diner, it had a sign on the door "White Trade Only" but we went anyway. We had heard that they had these big hamburgers, and we wanted one. There was a blonde, a blue-eyed girl behind the counter, a beauty. She asked what we wanted—real tough you know?—and when we ordered a hamburger, she said, "We don't sell to Mexicans," and she laughed when she said it. She enjoyed doing that, laughing

at us. We went out, but I was real mad, enraged.[28]

Squeezed Between Two Cultures

Widespread discrimination and rejection of Mexican American culture by Anglos resulted in an odd contradiction for young people growing up in the barrio. Mexican American youngsters attended American schools, saw the latest fashions, or watched Hollywood movies, but the lifestyles they heard about or viewed were unavailable to them. For many young people, the contradiction was obvious. Frances Esquibel Tywoniak notes:

I existed in two worlds, which I perceived to be divided by a distinct line of demarcation. On one side there was the sphere of experiences at school; these experiences had little, if anything to do with my real life.

. . . I was aware that most Mexicans were different in appearance from Anglos. I certainly could see that I was different. While I was not particularly dark . . . I had jet black hair,

Like these Mexican American students in Texas, most Mexican immigrant children attended segregated schools. The education they received at such schools was typically inferior to that of their Anglo peers.

similar to my father's, while some of the Anglo kids were much lighter in both hair and skin coloration.

This difference bothered me and even caused me some anguish. I knew or felt that I couldn't match the Anglo model of hairdos and clothing. The Anglo model was highly visible in school and the only model among teachers and in our school books.[29]

Not only did they find it difficult to fit into Anglo culture, young Mexican Amer-

---

The Zoot Suit and the Zoot Suit Riots

In August 1942 in Los Angeles, several young Mexican Americans were arrested in the stabbing death of another Mexican American, José Díaz. A sensational trial followed. Press reports described in lurid detail the supposed lifestyles and misdeeds of Mexican American youngsters who had adopted the mode of dress known as the zoot suit.

In the spring following the trial, sensationalized press coverage of alleged crimes by zoot-suit-clad Mexican American youths led Anglos, many of them uniformed navy sailors, to swarm through the streets of Los Angeles night after night, searching for zoot-suiters. The sailors and soldiers dragged young men out of streetcars and buses and stripped them, often cutting their long hair, beating them, and leaving them on the street.

These attacks began as street fighting, but escalated into a full-scale riot as police and sheriff's deputies stood by, allowing the servicemen to beat up the Mexican Americans and finally arresting the Mexican American youngsters for disturbing the peace. Members of the Mexican American community complained to local officials and the mayor in the weeks following the riot. But city officials praised the sailors, and the Los Angeles City Council even passed an ordinance that made wearing a zoot suit a misdemeanor.

Los Angeles police arrest a Mexican American man wearing a zoot suit.

icans found when they tried to do so, their parents often disapproved. For example, as historian Sarah Deutsch reports about New Mexico, "[younger] women wore high-heeled shoes and elaborate hats instead of shawls, danced modern dance steps, got permanents, and occasionally, in urban areas or villages with cars, went on dates while a mildly scandalized older generation looked on."[30]

The absence of parental approval aside, the conflict between wanting to be part of the majority culture and being rejected by that majority meant young Mexican Americans felt uncertain of where or whether they belonged. In response, during the 1940s many Mexican American young people in Southern California adopted their own style of dress. When they dressed up, they put on special clothing that set them apart from their Anglo peers. The teenage males wore long suits, broad-shouldered jackets and wide pleated pants, tight at the ankles, popularly called "zoot suits." They wore their hair swooped back over their heads in a ducktail, and often donned wide-brimmed hats pulled way down on their heads. Young women dressed in short skirts, long black stockings, and high, high heels, and wore bright lipstick and nail polish. Such styles upset adults, both Mexican American and Anglo. The so-called zoot-suiters' parents had never dressed like this, and much of the Los Angeles establishment saw the zoot suit as an outfit for wild hoodlums.

As young Mexican Americans were searching for a sense of belonging in Anglo society, the barrio represented a sanctuary for some. Yet most Mexican Americans hoped to capture the full promise of life in the United States. They wanted equal educational opportunities, the chance to live outside the barrio if they so desired, and to be able go to public swimming pools, restaurants, and dance halls without being rejected or refused service. They sought true inclusion into mainstream American society.

CHAPTER FOUR

Changing Times

Mexican Americans, confined to the barrio by continuing prejudice, longed to improve their situation. At the end of the nineteenth century they had formed mutual aid societies aimed at helping them to survive the injustices they faced. By the 1930s, however, the sons and daughters of these earlier arrivals sought to make a reality of the American creed that all people are created equal. Mexican Americans wanted to maintain their cultural heritage, but they wanted the same opportunities as Anglos for education, voting rights, employment, and public accommodations.

Even when, on the surface, they were included in Anglo society, Mexican Americans faced exclusion in unexpected ways. Dionicio Morales attended the local high school where he was one of just a few Mexican American students. In his autobiography he recalls an incident in which he suffered from outright discrimination even though he had achieved a measure of acceptance in his school. Morales describes how he, as a member of his high school band, attempted to join his fellow band members at a concert by a popular musician of the day:

> Our school dance band, which I had also joined, was bussed to the popular Ocean Park Dance Pavilion to

hear Henry Busey, the famous trumpet player, and his band. On the Friday evening of our arrival, the teacher lined us up to buy our tickets for the event. But when it came my turn to buy a ticket, the cashier told my teacher that Mexicans were not admitted to the Ocean Park Pavilion. The teacher simply went in with my fellow band members and told me that I was to wait outside until the group came out.[31]

Working for Reform

In the face of discrimination such as that experienced by Morales, Mexican Americans began organizing to eliminate social barriers. In Corpus Christi, Texas, in 1929, the League of United Latin American Citizens (LULAC) was established. Seeking to be thought of first as Americans, LULAC's organizers decided to adopt English as the group's official language. Still, while it desired to integrate Mexican Americans into the mainstream culture, LULAC members wanted to maintain pride in their unique heritage. Such dual cultural aims are included in LULAC's constitution, which states as its mission: "to develop within the membership of our race the best, purest and most perfect type of a true and loyal citizen of the United States of America. . . . We [nevertheless] solemnly declare once and for all to maintain a sincere and respectful reverence for our racial origin of which we are proud."[32]

The League of United Latin American Citizens (founding members pictured) was established to help Mexican immigrants integrate into American society while preserving their own identity.

LULAC fought a number of legal battles to help abolish segregated schools like this one in Texas.

LULAC's emphasis is on helping its members to adopt Anglo values and cultural traditions. It encourages immigrants to learn English, become U.S. citizens as soon as possible, get a good education, and get involved in community affairs. LULAC offers information on the American government and the U.S. Constitution in its meetings and publication, the *LULAC News*. Its many activities include raising money for college scholarships and charity projects, providing citizenship classes, and organizing voter registration drives. Although LULAC sees itself as a nonpolitical organization, it encourages Mexican Americans to vote in hopes of influencing local elections.

Because education is such an important part of LULAC's agenda, it became involved in legal attempts to desegregate schools. Such efforts met with only partial success, however. In 1930, for example, LULAC joined the lawsuit against the Del Rio Texas School District's segregation policies. Although the court ruled segregation on ethnic grounds was unconstitutional, it also held that language and academic skill could be grounds for assigning students to particular schools. It was an incomplete victory. LULAC, however, continued to work for equal opportunity of education. By the 1950s, LULAC widened its agenda to include other civil rights issues such as desegregating movie theaters and public swimming pools.

Similar groups followed LULAC's lead. One was the Mexican American Movement (MAM) established in 1938 by young people in Los Angeles to improve educational opportunities for Mexican American youth. (MAM dissolved in 1950.) MAM's long-term goal was to develop a civil consciousness in Mexican Americans through education. It published a newspaper, the *Mexican Voice*, and held conferences bringing young people together to discuss the problems and possible solutions for the inequality they faced. MAM believed that success came with education, and a college degree would bring about acceptance for Mexican Americans in the United States. In addition, MAM members maintained that with a high school diploma or college degree young people would increase their understanding of life outside the barrio. José Rodriques, a member of MAM, wrote in the *Mexican Voice*, "Education is the only tool which will raise our influence, command the respect of the rich class, and enable us to mingle in their social, political and religious life." He added, "Education means a complete knowledge of yourself, a good knowledge of your fellowmen and a thorough knowledge of the world in which you live. . . . EDUCATION is our *only weapon*."[33]

While MAM and LULAC promoted education as essential to social acceptance and civil reform, the Spanish-speaking Peoples Congress (*El Congreso de Los Pueblos de Habla Española*), founded in 1938, adopted broader goals and more radical approaches to achieving them. It hoped to gain specific civil rights for all people of Mexican origin. The congress wanted workers to get fair wages and equal treatment, and so it began union organizing. The congress also complained to local officials about cases in California where police brutality was used against Mexican Americans. It offered counseling services to immigrants and advised noncitizens regarding the intricacies of the naturalization process. In addition, like other groups, the Spanish-speaking Peoples Congress stressed the importance for Mexican American youth of obtaining a good education. The congress spoke out against the rundown facilities given to Mexican American students in the segregated Los Angeles school system and complained to federal officials about discrimination in employment in the defense industries during the early days of World War II.

The Door Begins to Open

Despite the efforts of organizations such as LULAC, MAM, and the Spanish-speaking Peoples Congress, discrimination largely continued. Yet in 1941, when the United States was plunged into World War II, half a million Mexican Americans—laborers, farmers, students, small business owners, and farmworkers—responded, enlisting in all branches of the armed services. As historian Ronald Takaki explains,

The war offered Mexican Americans a chance to claim the United States as their country and their right to equality. . . . One of the defenders, soldier Anthony Navarro, explained: "We wanted to prove that while our cultural ties were deeply rooted in Mexico, our home was here in this country." . . . Military service was serving as a path toward a brighter future.[34]

Yet these Mexican Americans saw the irony in risking their lives for a nation that discriminated against them. Raul Morin, a World War II veteran from Los Angeles, was anxious to serve his country but like others he felt conflicted. Morin recalls asking himself,

Why fight for America when you have not been treated as an American? Do

During World War II, half a million Mexican Americans fought in the armed forces despite the fact that they continued to face discrimination at home.

you really think that in the event the United States wins the war the Mexicans will be given better treatment? Are you really ready to lay down your life for this country? . . . [But nothing could] make me change the feeling I had for my home in America, the country where I was born. All we wanted was a chance to prove how loyal and American we were.[35]

In combat Mexican Americans proved themselves not just loyal to their country, but exceptionally brave. They earned seventeen Congressional Medals of Honor—more Medals of Honor in proportion to their population than any other ethnic group in the United States. Despite the obvious willingness of Mexican Americans to risk their lives for their country, discrimination at first continued on the home front, especially in the defense industries. For example, a confidential report made in the early years of the war by the federal government's Office of War Information stated: "The airplane industry of Southern California has been consistent in asserting that it does not discriminate, but payrolls show almost no Mexican(s) [Americans] employed. One plant personnel man stated that his company would employ them if they were not 'too racial'—'too dark.'"[36]

Similarly, at the beginning of the war there were no people with Spanish surnames employed in the Los Angeles shipyards. But the need for workers in the war industries eventually forced open the doors, and by 1943 there were seventeen thousand Mexican Americans working in the shipyards. Many, both women and men, found new opportunities in steel and ammunition plants as well as building aircraft or ships.

Mexican Americans quickly took advantage of the chance for good jobs. "Prior to the war," recalls Natalie Martinez Sterling, "the only jobs available to young Mexican women were non-skilled types of occupations such as making cardboard boxes and sewing clothes. The war allowed us job opportunities as sales clerks and defense workers. The government was actually training us with job skills that would help us after the war."[37]

Along with good jobs, the defense industry offered the possibility for better wages. Felicia Ruiz remembers,

During the depression, the only jobs available to young Mexican American women were limited primarily to sewing and laundry work, hotel maids, and as domestics [house keepers]. These jobs were both physically demanding and paid very little. When the war broke out, defense jobs were all of a sudden open to us because of the labor shortage with the men off to war. Many of us left these menial jobs into highly skilled occupations with good to excellent pay with overtime.[38]

War Veterans

The war brought changes that affected Mexican Americans serving in the military as well as those on the home front. Men and women in the armed services learned about the world outside the barrio.

Military service gave Mexican Americans a chance to get to know Anglos. Seventeen-year-old Cesar Chavez, who later became a union organizer, was in San Diego in boot camp when he realized other ethnic groups faced prejudice similar to what Mexican Americans faced. Chavez later said, "I saw this white kid fighting, because someone had called him a Polak and I found out he was Polish and hated the word Polak. He fought every time he heard it. I began to learn something, that others suffered, too."[39]

As Mexican Americans got to know other ethic groups so, too, did Anglos get a chance to meet and work with Mexican Americans. And as a result, many found their prejudices challenged by these experiences. For example, in his basic training at Camp Roberts, California, Raul Morin describes how he met soldiers,

who had never associated or had ever seen a Mexican [American] before. We [Mexican Americans] were amused with the description they gave and the concept they had of a Mexican [American] back in their hometowns. Walt Musick, from South Dakota, was being very frank when he told us, "The only Mexicans we ever saw back home were those that worked on the railroad and lived in section houses. I had always heard that they were not to be trusted, and if you turned your back to them they would knife you in the back. But these fellows I have known here in [Camp] Roberts are just like other Americans."[40]

If the war experiences helped transform Anglo veterans' attitudes about Mexican Americans, returning Mexican American veterans also came back with new ideas about their rightful place in American society. As Raul Morin writes:

For the returning Mexican-American veteran, things *were* different and furthermore he did not want to find things the way he had left them. . . . For too long we had been like outsiders. It had never made very much difference to us and we hardly noticed until we got back from overseas. How could we have played such a prominent part as Americans over there and now have to go back living as outsiders as before? . . . How long had we been missing out on benefits derived as an American citizen?[41]

Veterans and the American GI Forum

When the war ended in 1945, Mexican American veterans returned to civilian life determined to change their status. Having risked their lives for their country, they decided the time had come to fight for the rights they were entitled to as citizens. To begin the reform process, Mexican American vets formed the American GI Forum. The GI Forum developed plans to desegregate public schools, movie theaters,

Hector Perez Garcia (center) marches with members of the GI Forum to demand a fair minimum wage for Texas farm workers.

swimming pools, and parks. Led by Hector Perez Garcia, who had served as a combat surgeon in the war, the GI Forum encouraged all members of the Mexican American community to get involved in ending segregation by complaining to local officials and government administrators about discrimination. It encouraged citizens to register to vote and to vote for those politicians who supported integration. The GI Forum also joined LULAC in bringing school desegregation cases before the courts.

Some veterans also found help under provisions of the GI Bill. Passed by Congress, the GI Bill provided money for veterans to attend college and low interest loans to buy homes or start businesses. As a result of this legislation, although political equality was not yet a reality, by the 1950s significant numbers of Mexican Americans obtained training for professional and technical jobs as well as skills needed for managerial and clerical positions. So it was that some Mexican Americans, even though they often saw jobs go to less-qualified Anglo applicants, entered the middle class. For many others, in spite of the GI Forum's efforts, joining the armed services remained the only way of getting away from the barrio, bias in the workplace, or finding access to good educational opportunity.

Grassroots Organizations

Although social and economic gains had come for some, true equality had not yet been achieved. In the face of continued discrimination, middle-class Mexican Americans formed civic unity leagues, believing improvements could come if they worked in their local communities. They developed programs to get Mexican Americans to learn English, American history, and to vote. In California towns with large Mexican American populations like Chino, Pomona, San Bernardino, and Ontario, unity leagues convinced Mexican Americans to run for local offices, and some of them won.

Organizing at the grassroots level seemed the best way to improve local conditions. Edward R. Roybal, a college-educated World War II vet, used his energy and convictions to put together the Community Service Organization (CSO) in Los Angeles along with Fred Ross. Ross had been trained by Saul Alinsky, a Chicago social activist who headed the Industrial Areas Foundation, to teach barrio residents how to work for their rights and develop political power. The CSO formed self-help groups of Mexican Americans in the barrios and began community organizing. The CSO's efforts focused on using the power of the ballot to effect change, and in Los Angeles, CSO volunteers set out to register barrio voters. In 1949 Ross and Roybal developed a successful campaign to get Roybal elected to the Los Angeles City Council—the first Mexican American to serve on the council since 1881. And so a change began in the city with one of the largest Spanish-speaking populations in the United States.

During the 1950s, CSO moved out to other towns, and soon became the most active Mexican American civil rights or-

Edward R. Roybal: Political Pioneer

When Edward R. Roybal was growing up in a Los Angeles barrio no one dreamed he would someday live a life in service to others. He graduated from Roosevelt High School during the depth of the Great Depression and since it was impossible to find a job he joined the Civilian Conservation Corp (CCC), helping to plant trees and improve parks. Later Roybal attended UCLA and earned a degree in accounting. After graduation, Roybal realized that a large number of Mexican Americans suffered from tuberculosis, and he volunteered to test children for the disease. This led him to work as a public health educator for the Los Angeles County Tuberculosis and Health Association. When World War II began in 1941, he signed up for military service, but when he returned to civilian life he again went into public health.

Along with Fred Ross, Roybal founded the Community Service Organization (CSO) to help organize Mexican Americans in the barrios. As a health care worker, he saw that only through exercising their vote could poor people improve their lives. Roybal ran for the Los Angeles City Council in 1947 and was defeated. But then CSO registered over twelve thousand new voters, and in 1949 Roybal became the first Mexican American to win election to the council in the twentieth century. During the next thirteen years, he championed community rights for health care.

In 1962 Roybal was elected to the U.S. House of Representatives—only the second Mexican American to gain national office. He spent the next thirty years working for civil rights, human rights, bilingual education, health care, and making attempts to improve the lives of all people. In 1977 he stepped down from elected office at the age of seventy-seven years, but he kept laboring for the rights of Americans to decent health care.

ganization in California and Arizona. But the agricultural sectors had experienced none of the changes that were taking place in the rest of society; many field hands still lived in circumstances that afforded them few rights or services. In its efforts to address the needs of Mexican Americans who continued to work in the fields where America's food was grown, the CSO served as a training ground for a new generation of labor activists.

Cesar Chavez and the United Farm Workers

Since the beginning of the twentieth century, agricultural workers had joined various unions. None of these had achieved lasting results because commercial growers wielded tremendous power. These individuals owned thousands of acres of farmland, giving them control of the job market. Furthermore, they were able to defeat most unions by importing guest workers from Mexico, using strikebreakers, blacklisting union organizers, or hiring vigilantes to keep away picketers. The result was that conditions for field laborers had hardly improved since the 1930s and farmworkers were some of the poorest people in the United States.

The CSO's importance to the nascent labor movement began in 1952 when Ross went to Delano, a farming community in California, to help establish a group. There, Ross met Cesar Chavez, a shy twenty-four-year-old vet who following the war had returned to agricultural work. Ross convinced Chavez to help him organize farmworkers. At first, Chavez picked apricots during the day, and at night he registered voters and set up English

Cesar Chavez

For many Mexican Americans Cesar Chavez's life represents a model of selfless activism. He was born on his family's farm in Arizona in 1927 and lived there until he was ten years old. During the Great Depression, the family lost the land, and Cesar and his family traveled to California as poor migrant workers. Cesar picked crops in the fields, orchards, and vineyards beside his family. They sometimes lived out of their car as they moved from farm to farm, harvesting America's food. By the time Cesar finished eighth grade and went to work fulltime, he had attended thirty-seven schools.

During World War II, Chavez went into the navy, and in the years following his return, he began a struggle for the rights of the poor farmworkers. First he worked with the Community Service Organization (CSO) and later formed the United Farm Workers (UFW).

Although some people say Chavez was the father of the Chicano movement because he was the first Mexican American activist to gain national recognition, he remained dedicated all his life to *la*

Causa, the cause of migrant farm labor. Chavez died in 1993, having done all he could to improve the lives of the poor people who labor in the fields.

Cesar Chavez dedicated his adult life to improving conditions for migrant workers.

classes. In 1958 Chavez became the paid director of the CSO and led meetings of fellow farmworkers.

Within a few years, however, Chavez came to believe that even more than political power, Mexican American farmworkers needed an organization to help end their exploitation by large growers. Most workers continued to work long hours in the fields without toilet facilities or adequate drinking water, and they were forced to use the short-handled hoe as they stooped to tend the crops. Although child labor laws had been passed by the U.S. Congress, state and federal officials rarely enforced such laws. Many children still labored in the fields alongside their parents and moved with them from farm to farm, following the growing season. The housing given to migrant workers often consisted of old shacks, chicken coops, or barracks. Structures lacked indoor plumbing, cooking facilities, electricity, or any source of heat. Despite enduring all these hardships, workers earned barely enough money to get by.

It was these conditions Chavez wanted to change. In 1962, taking his own savings from his years as CSO director, Chavez, along with his wife Helen and another activist named Dolores Huerta, started the National Farm Workers Association (NFWA). Chavez and Huerta worked month in and month out, traveling from farm to farm throughout the valleys of California signing up union members. By 1965 they had recruited more than twelve hundred farm workers. In September of that year the Agricultural Workers Organizing Committee (AWOC), a Filipino union associated with the AFL-CIO, decided to strike the grape fields of Delano demanding higher wages. The leaders of the AWOC asked Chavez and the NFWA to join them.

Chavez was skeptical of the advisability of a strike, believing the NFWA needed more time to grow, but when he attended the meeting and found two thousand workers shouting "Huelga! Huelga!"[42] (Strike! Strike!), he agreed to join them. With Chavez as the president, the workers soon formed the United Farm Workers (UFW). After a few weeks, two vineyards agreed to pay increases and recognized the workers' right to bargain through a union. The pickers went back to the harvest at those vineyards. But most large growers refused. Chavez knew he had to find other ways to oppose the powerful commercial landowners. The UFW started strikes and picketed the fields, but in November 1965, the union called for an international boycott of grapes.

To dramatize the plight of poor farmworkers, the next spring Chavez led a three-hundred-mile march from Delano to Sacramento, California. Hundreds of people across the nation heard of the migrants' problems and came to join the march. Students, nuns, ministers, doctors, lawyers, and farm laborers all walked together to the state capital. The word got out, "Don't buy grapes." As more people boycotted grapes, more growers signed with the UFW. By 1970 the UFW had signed agreements with more than two dozen growers in Delano. The UFW went on to the Salinas Valley to organize lettuce pickers there. Concerning the many hard

Dolores Huerta: Her Work Is Where Her Heart Is

Dolores Huerta was born in a small mining town in northern New Mexico in 1930, but she grew up in Stockton, California, in a neighborhood that included Filipinos, Japanese, Chinese, and Jews, as well as Mexican Americans. Huerta would later say that this ethnically diverse community helped her appreciate a variety of people.

When Huerta finished high school, she went to college and earned a teaching certificate. Soon she realized, however, she needed to do something for destitute migrant field-workers. She went to work for the Community Service Organization (CSO) and registered Mexican Americans to vote, enrolled them in English and citizenship classes, and tried to help them any way she could. Huerta believed what agricultural workers lacked was a union to bargain for fair pay so they could buy what they needed to live decently. She and Cesar Chavez

cofounded the farmworkers union. Chavez was the president, and Huerta was elected first vice president of the United Farm Workers (UFW) in 1973.

Huerta remained a powerful force in the union and vigorously led workers on the picket lines, organized the eastern grape boycott, and talked for hours on end to get fair contracts for farm labor. In 1970 she bargained with the commercial growers to pay higher wages, make contributions to a health fund and medical clinic, and even limit the use of dangerous pesticides. In her lifelong commitment to the union she has performed a variety of tasks—including fund-raising, contract negotiating, testifying before government committees, walking picket lines, marching down the streets of San Francisco, and training other union members. In her seventies, Huerta continues to organize for the union long past the age when most people retire.

years of trying to gain fair wages and union contracts for California farm-workers, Chavez later said, "Our struggle is not easy, we are poor. But we have our bodies and spirits and the justice of our cause as our weapons."[43] While Chavez received much attention for the successes of the UFW, many others, including Fred Ross and Dolores Huerta worked tirelessly for *la Causa*. And there continued to be successes and defeats for those who worked at growing America's food.

While the postwar years brought improvements to the lives of many Mexican Americans, the promise of American justice for all remained unfulfilled for the vast majority. Although gains had been made in jobs, local politics, and some local communities, few Mexican Americans had gained national leadership roles or election to national office. It was the youth movements and rising activism of the 1960s that brought new vigor to the struggle for true equality.

CHAPTER FIVE

The Chicano Movement

The 1960s were a time of social and political agitation, especially among young people, all across the United States. Emboldened by the reforms achieved by African Americans, young Mexican Americans asserted pride in their cultural heritage and insisted that slow, small political and social reforms would no longer be satisfactory. Furthermore, many came to believe the goal of assimilation into Anglo society was unrealistic. These activists instead chose to focus on their cultural uniqueness. If Mexican Americans were to gain power, these activists said, all people of Mexican origin needed to come together, and this unity could be achieved by recalling and celebrating their cultural roots.

A Place in American Society

Taking their cue from the experience of African Americans as they fought for civil rights, younger Mexican Americans rejected the idea of reform coming at the cost of their cultural heritage. Instead, they sought to celebrate their cultural uniqueness by calling themselves "Chicanos," a word derived from the ancient Aztec name for Mexico, "Meshica." The newly born Chicano movement would work for civil and political rights and an end to social and cultural discrimination in America.

Demanding Educational Change

Most of the Chicano movement's activities began in Mexican American communities or on high school and college campuses. As Chicano activists made plans, they recognized one of the most pressing needs was to increase educational achievement among young Chicanos, who in U.S. cities experienced the highest school dropout rates of any ethnic group. Their average education attainment was 8.1 years of school, lower than other non-white students and about four years below that of Anglos.

To Chicano activists, the reasons for the achievement gap was clear. In cities like Los Angeles, young people had continued to be educated in barrio schools with watered-down curriculum, poorly trained teachers, and deteriorating facilities. Little had changed from the 1950s, and one woman remembers that during her days in the barrio at Abraham Lincoln High School, "They didn't teach me anything at school. The teachers didn't care, . . . We never had homework, which I think is bad. We did embroidery."[44]

Another person who felt the inadequacy of the East Los Angeles Schools was Salvador "Sal" Castro, a Korean War veteran who had attended college on the GI Bill and had become a teacher in East Los Angeles. What Castro saw upset him. There were no Mexican American administrators, few teachers of Mexican origin, and nothing in his mind to make Chicano students "feel part of the program. . . . I knew there was something wrong about the schools before I walked in," said Castro. "Mexican kids were not encouraged to go to college, and there were very few Latino kids in the Student Council. They were being systematically excluded."[45]

Working with a group known as United Mexican American Students (UMAS), Castro and other reform-

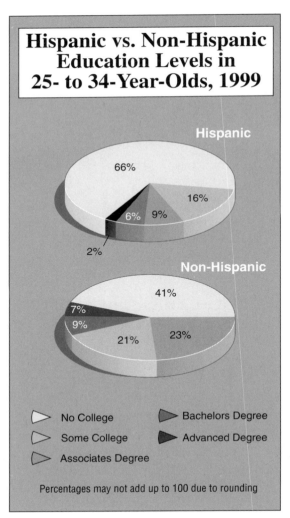

Hispanic vs. Non-Hispanic Education Levels in 25- to 34-Year-Olds, 1999

Hispanic

66%

16%

6% 9%

2%

Non-Hispanic

41%

7%

9%

21%

23%

▷ No College ▷ Bachelors Degree
▷ Some College ▶ Advanced Degree
▷ Associates Degree

Percentages may not add up to 100 due to rounding

minded people from the area decided Chicano youths would hold a nonviolent protest against the Los Angeles school system to draw attention to their educational needs. On the morning of March 3, 1968, Castro and more than a thousand Chicano students walked out of their classes at Abraham Lincoln High School. They met UMAS students and community activists who handed them picket signs. These signs carried phrases such as "Education not Contempt," "Chicano Power," "Viva La Raza" (Long Live the People), and "We Demand Schools That Teach." A student strike committee settled on thirty-six demands to put before the school board, including freedom of speech, classes on Mexican American history, and more Mexican American teachers and administrators. News of the strike spread quickly and before long over four thousand students from five high schools in East Los Angeles had joined the strike. The police moved in to arrest the thirteen strike leaders, including Castro, on charges of disturbing the peace. But despite such tactics, the strike eventually spread across the state and twenty thousand students went out on strike.

Dial Torgerson of the *Los Angeles Times* called the strike "The Birth of Brown Power."[46] It was the first mass protest by Mexican Americans in the United States against racism, and its impact reached across the nation. Within a few months student walkouts and boycotts had spread to other California schools and on to Texas, New Mexico, Arizona, Michigan, and Colorado.

Student Movements

In the weeks following the walkout, UMAS explained how the organization saw its role as an agent for social change. The UMAS newsletter stated,

> We have begun to recognize our role as an organizational agent through which Chicano students are able to recognize themselves as Mexicans and take pride in it. We are the avant-garde [forerunners] of the young Mexican American liberation movement. . . . We recognize ourselves as a generation of doers as well as thinkers. . . . We are the agents of progress and unity. We demand social justice for a people too long oppressed.[47]

About this same time, other organizations were formed to effect even more basic reforms. One such group was the Mexican American Youth Organization (MAYO) founded in 1967 at Saint Mary's College in San Antonio, Texas, by Saint Mary's graduate José Angel Gutierrez and former migrant worker Mario Compean. They hoped to organize students and community members to change the school systems to reflect the needs of Chicano students. MAYO also wanted to make Mexican Americans in Texas more aware of their rights and to help entire Mexican American communities get involved in politics. MAYO took a leading role in organizing various school walkouts in Texas. Its provocative language and actions frightened more conservative Mexican Americans, but the organization's radical

Bert Corona: A Man Without Borders

In his lifetime Bert Corona was active trying to improve the lives of the Mexican American community. He worked with Cesar Chavez, with youth organizations and political groups, and tried to help all workers, documented and undocumented, get the social services and fair wages they needed to live above the poverty level.

Born in El Paso, Texas, in 1918, Corona moved to California with his family and grew up there. Later he attended the University of Southern California. During college he worked as a stevedore at the Los Angeles port and it was then he first joined a union. Corona rose to the presidency of Local 26 of the International Longshoremen and Warehousemen's Union in 1941. Because he had headed many successful union drives for the Congress of Industrial Organizations (CIO), Chavez asked Corona to get Mexican workers to support the United Farm Workers (UFW) grape boycott and strike. So Corona went to the fields and even traveled to Mexico, asking workers to refuse jobs left vacant by striking UFW members. And most followed his instructions.

During the 1960s, Corona worked on immigration and served as a consultant to the U.S. Labor Department. He was deeply concerned about the poor treatment of Mexican-origin workers and organized Centro de Acción Social Autónoma (CASA), or Center for Socially Autonomous Action, in Los Angeles. It was Corona's goal for CASA to link Mexican and Mexican American workers in one group, and he tried to get Chicanos to support undocumented workers in their drive for economic and social justice.

By the time Corona died in 1995 he had influenced almost every issue important to the Mexican Americans in the twentieth century.

image attracted high school and college students to its ranks.

Another organization, the Crusade for Justice, sought to inspire youth by raising both ethnic and political awareness. The Crusade's founder, Rudolfo "Corky" Gonzalez, had been a professional boxer and later a Democratic Party organizer. But it was Gonzalez's poem *I Am Joaquin/Yo Soy Joaquin* that really fired young Chicanos' imaginations. The epic poem tells of Joaquin, whose journey takes him to historical events from Aztec, Mexican, and American history, and it speaks of the Chicano struggle for finding a place in the world. Young Mexican Americans saw in the poem the story of their own search for identity.

After hearing the poem, Chicanos decided they would no longer sit by and take what was given to them by Anglos. In Denver, in 1969, the Crusade for Justice sponsored a conference of young activists from all over the country. At the conference Gonzalez told those gathered that their sense of themselves as a nation [a special people] had failed to be,

> formed into an image people can see. Until now it has been a dream. . . . It has been my job to create a reality out of the dream. . . . Everybody in the barrios is a nationalist. . . . [I]t doesn't matter if he's middle-class, *a vendido*, a sellout, or what his politics may be. He'll come back home to La Raza [the People], to his heart. . . . We are awakening people, an emerging nation, a new breed.[48]

Cheers rang out at his words, and excitement ran high as the student activists set about to define their goals. The outcome of the conference was a document known as El Plan Espiritual de Aztlán, (the Spiritual Plan of Aztlán), which listed specific ways to improve people's lives and to connect all Chicanos to their Mexican roots.

El Plan Espiritual de Aztlán and Chicano Studies

The Plan reminded followers of their shared history and identity. As historians Richard Griswold del Castillo and Arnoldo De León say,

> El Plan Espiritual de Aztlán defined all Mexican-origin people in the United States as La Raza Bronze (the Bronze People), a Mestizo people proud of their Indian roots. . . . The students sought to unify all Mexi-

cans, whether immigrant or native-born: "With our heart in our hands and our hands in the soil, we declare the independence of our mestizo nation. We are a bronze people with a bronze culture. Before all North America, before all our brothers in the bronze continent, we are a nation, we are a union of free pueblos, we are Aztlán."[49]

The students followed these bold words by planning a conference at the University

Aztlán

The Aztec of Mexico traced their origins to Aztlán, a land somewhere in the north. The Aztec chronicles describe how the Aztec were forced to leave this land and after much wandering, settled in the Valley of Mexico.

In the 1960s and 1970s, when a young group of Mexican Americans attempted to show pride in their ethnic heritage, they used this legendary homeland of Aztlán as a cultural reminder of their Mexican ancestry and origin. The Aztec tales describe an ancestral homeland somewhere north of Mexico City, and many people believe it was the American Southwest.

By recalling Aztlán, Chicanos wanted to bring a sense of the common history of both U.S. citizens and Mexican immigrants.

of California at Santa Barbara designed to develop strategies for bringing their agenda to college and university campuses. That agenda, worked out with the help of another organization, the Aztlán Chicano Student Movement (MEChA), included demands that colleges offer more scholarships to Chicanos, hire more Chicano faculty, and start programs, departments, or courses on Mexican American history, literature, and culture. The overall goal was for Chicanos to be treated in academia in the same way as other immigrant groups such as the Germans, French, Italians, Irish, and English. As a result of MEChA and other groups' efforts, over the next decades, college programs, research centers, courses, and departments of Chicano or Latino studies were established.

La Raza Unida

Although colleges and universities began to respond to the concerns of Chicano students and national organizations worked to increase awareness of Mexican Americans' contributions to American life, many of the young activists still felt excluded from the political process. What they needed, some Chicanos felt, was their own political party, since there were still few Mexican Americans in national or state offices. As a result, in 1970 José Gutierrez, cofounder of the Mexican American Youth Organization (MAYO), gathered over three hundred people in Texas and formed La Raza Unida (the United Peoples) Party. The party was hoping to attract older Mexican Americans as well as young people. In several poor towns along the Mexican-Texas border, La Raza Unida ran candidates who won local elections. In 1972 and 1974, La Raza Unida even ran a candidate, Ramsey Muñiz, for governor of Texas, and he gained a significant number of votes each time. Although La Raza Unida won some local races, membership in it faded by the end of the 1970s. Political activists, however, had gained skills and knowledge that they would apply in the years to come.

Gaining Recognition

The energy generated by the Chicano movement focused national attention on the needs of Mexican Americans for economic improvement as well as on their unique cultural contributions. This attention resulted in money and support coming in from new sources. In 1968, for example, with the aid of a grant from the Ford Foundation, The Southwest Council of La Raza was established in San Antonio, Texas. In 1973 it moved to Washington, D.C., and became known as the National Council of La Raza. Its overall goal is to end discrimination against Mexican Americans and to ensure their inclusion in all facets of American life.

Mexican American Legal Defense and Education Fund

Although most Mexican Americans wanted to foster ethnic pride, some older Mexican Americans feared the activists and the radical methods of the younger generation. All agreed, however, that seg-

The Chicano Moratorium and Ruben Salazar

The organizers of the 1968 Los Angeles school strike helped to assemble the first mass protest event of the Chicano movement in 1970. The organizers realized Mexican Americans were 10 percent of the population, but their people made up 20 percent of the casualities in the Vietnam War. For this and other reasons, many Mexican Americans opposed the war in Vietnam. Community organizers brought together Catholic action groups, student action groups, Campaign for Justice participants, Vietnam vets, and middle-class community people to protest the ongoing war in Vietnam and to call for a moratorium to the fighting.

A crowd of well over twenty thousand marched through the streets of Los Angeles on August 29, 1970. The parade ended in Laguna Park. Soon about five hundred police officers surrounded the park and ordered those already at the park to leave. Rioting began when hundreds of deputy sheriffs rushed into the crowd clubbing participants and firing tear gas. Panic erupted and rioting led to vandalism on Whittier Boulevard along the parade route. The violence ended hours later with the arrest of hundreds of marchers and the death of three people.

One of those killed was Ruben Salazar, the popular news director for the Los Angeles TV station KMEX, the local Spanish-language station, and a veteran journalist for the *Los Angeles Times.* In his reporting Salazar had often been critical of the brutality of the police department. At the time of his death, Salazar was sitting in a bar along Whittier Boulevard when a deputy sheriff shot a tear gas canister into the building, hitting Salazar in the head and killing him.

Many questions arose about the investigation of Salazar's death. The coroner's report condemned the moratorium, which it had no authority to do, and then ruled Salazar's death "accidental." But because of the poor handling of the inquiry, many Chicanos believe the police had set out to silence Salazar.

regation and discrimination had to end. The effort to bring about reform found a different approach in the late 1960s as Mexican Americans began graduating from the nation's law schools. These young lawyers graduated with a strong social consciousness, and they looked to the U.S. legal system and the courts as a means to bring civil and political justice to the Chicano community.

Gathering in 1968, young lawyers organized the Mexican American Legal Defense and Education Fund (MALDEF). One of the major concerns of MALDEF was to ensure equality of opportunity for Mexican Americans through education.

As a result, it brought lawsuits against cities and school districts that continued to discriminate against Chicanos. In case after case, MALDEF sued those school systems that showed bias against immigrants and Mexican Americans. One of the most significant of its early victories was the *Cisneros v. Corpus Christi Independent School District* case in 1970, which determined that Mexican Americans could be considered as an ethnic group for the purposes of desegregating schools. Just as it was no longer acceptable to segregate African American students, now it would be illegal to segregate Mexican Americans.

In Texas MALDEF found many districts gave more money to predominantly Anglo schools than to predominantly Mexican American schools. So in 1989 MALDEF filed a suit, which resulted in the state legislature eventually changing its financial formula to assure equal monies for the education of Chicanos.

Besides education, MALDEF was concerned with civil rights, especially voting rights. Young lawyers worked with the Southwest Voter Registration Education Project (SWVRP) that was founded in 1974 by Willie Velasquez. SWVRP hoped to bring political power to Mexican American communities by encouraging the election of those politicians who favored equality of opportunity for Chicanos. Working with SWVRP, MALDEF filed suits proving that discrimination had been practiced against Chicanos, using various methods to exclude Mexican American voters from gaining political power. Because of the efforts of MALDEF, in 1975 the Voting Rights Act was extended to require ballots to be printed in Spanish for voters who requested them.

The New Politician

With the inspiration of the Chicano movement and the triumphs in courts, Mexican American voting power increased during the 1970s and 1980s. While Henry B. Gonzales had become the first Mexican American from Texas elected to the Congress in 1960 and Edward R. Roybal had won election to the House of Representatives from California in 1962, it took until the 1980s before real power came to Mexican American voters.

As barriers to Mexican Americans' participation in politics fell in cities, towns, and states, Chicanos found success at the polls; others gained appointment to national offices. An example of local success was Henry Cisneros, who was elected mayor of San Antonio in 1981. Cisneros, whose father had been a migrant worker, went on to serve in the cabinet as secretary of the Department of Housing and Urban Development (HUD) under President Bill Clinton. Another prominent politician, Federico Peña, once a lawyer for MALDEF, won election in 1983 as mayor of Denver. He was just thirty-six years old and one of the youngest people to be elected mayor in the United States. Later, he became secretary of the Department of Transportation and after that secretary of the Department of Energy. After his election in 1988, President George H.W. Bush, chose Manuel Lujan Jr. as secretary of the interior and Lauro F. Cavazos as secretary of education.

By the beginning of the twenty-first century, four Mexican Americans had won election as state governors: in Arizona, Raul Castro, and in New Mexico, Jerry Apodaca, Toney Anaya, and Bill Richardson. Richardson also served as the U.S. ambassador to the United Nations and the secretary of energy under Clinton.

While Mexican American men gained offices in the years following the Chicano movement, few women held leadership roles. But Gloria Molina was determined to speak out for women and her community. While she was a college student in Los Angeles during the 1960s, the Chicano movement inspired Molina as it had so many other young people. In later years she worked for Mexican American politicians in California before running for the State Assembly herself in 1982. Her decision met with opposition from even her coworkers, however. When Molina decided

Henry Cisneros gained political power first as mayor of San Antonio, Texas, and later as a member of President Clinton's cabinet.

to run, many of the minority men she had worked with thought a woman candidate "was out of the question. That did motivate me," she said later. "That made me very determined [to run and win]."[50]

Molina was the first Mexican American woman elected to the state legislature and five years later she became the first Mexican American woman elected to the Los Angeles City Council. Afterward she said the men who influence Southern California's growing Latino community "are [now] going to be more responsive to my concerns."[51]

Throughout her political career, Molina worked on issues important to her community such as health, education, women's rights, gangs, and services for the poor. Her efforts made her popular with women and with non–Mexican American voters as well. As a result, she won election to the Los Angeles County Board of Supervisors in a city with the largest Mexican American population. As

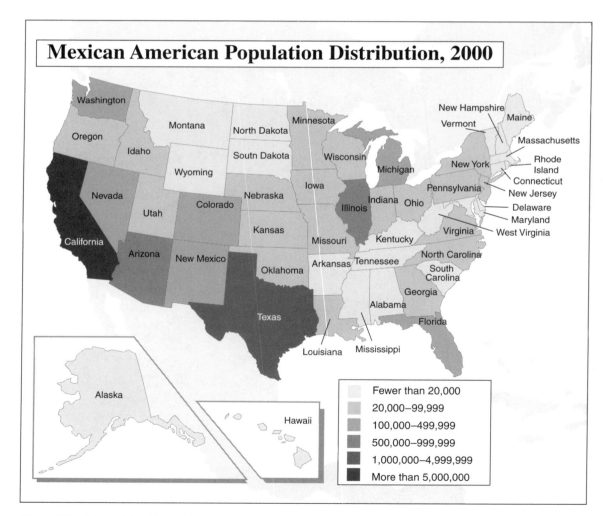

Mexican American Population Distribution, 2000

Washington
Oregon
Idaho
Montana
North Dakota
Minnesota
New Hampshire
Vermont
Maine
Massachusetts
Nevada
Wyoming
Soutn Dakota
Wisconsin
Michigan
New York
Rhode Island
Connecticut
Utah
Colorado
Nebraska
Iowa
Pennsylvania
New Jersey
California
Arizona
New Mexico
Kansas
Illinois
Indiana
Ohio
Delaware
Maryland
West Virginia
Oklahoma
Missouri
Kentucky
Virginia
Arkansas
Tennessee
North Carolina
South Carolina
Texas
Georgia
Alabama
Florida
Louisiana
Mississippi

Alaska
Hawaii

Fewer than 20,000
20,000–99,999
100,000–499,999
500,000–999,999
1,000,000–4,999,999
More than 5,000,000

the first Mexican American county supervisor in Los Angeles in more than a century she told the press, "I'm looking to work with them [the board members] in a partnership to bring about some changes. . . . I can't go into the Board of Supervisors and start acting like them. I did not get elected to meet their needs. I was elected to meet the needs of the people in the First District. . . . Politics have changed."[52]

Although Gloria Molina came to be called a trailblazer, others continued to make gains. Since the Chicano movement began, several Mexican Americans have won congressional elections. By 1976 Spanish-speaking politicians in Washington, D.C., formed the Hispanic Congressional Caucus to work on issues vital to their communities such as immigration, police brutality, bilingual education, and discrimination. While the caucus represented more than just Mexican Americans, its commitment to work together came as a direct result of the opportunities and civil rights gained during the years of the Chicano movement.

A Question of Identity

The Mexican Americans coming of age during the 1960s used the word "Chicano" to designate their ethnic group, but the older generation often preferred to be called "Mexican American." Many, like Juan Cadena, felt the term "Chicano" failed to reflect who they were: "I don't use the word *chicano*. I'm not comfortable with it because that's not the way I learned to use *chicano*. . . . The first time I used *chicano* was in the forties [1940s]. To us, *chicano* was like the kids now use *dude*."[53]

Gradually, many in the Chicano movement came to believe they had much in common with others whose native tongue was Spanish. Although some cultural differences existed, these were less significant than the common experience of wanting to feel pride in their Latin roots and the Spanish language.

As a result of such realizations, some Chicanos suggested their community should include all people of Spanish-speaking heritage. The word "Hispanic" had been used in the past and now some even used "Latino." Both of these expressions had much broader meaning than just "Mexican American." In addition to Mexican Americans, these terms include people of Puerto Rican and Cuban descent, as well as anyone else whose ancestors had come from Spain or from South America and Central America.

By the 1980s, new waves of immigrants from Latin American and Mexico made Latinos the largest group of immigrants. In 2000 the U.S. Census Bureau estimated there were approximately 35 million Latinos in the country, including the island of Puerto Rico, and by 2003 Latinos were the largest non-Anglo population. Although those of Mexican descent represent approximately 60 percent of the "Latinos" or "Hispanics," these terms link together people from different cultures. Just as the term "Mexican American" or "Chicano" represents individuals with quite different backgrounds and lives, so, too, does the Latino or Hispanic community represent a diversity of individuals.

The efforts of the Chicano movement resulted in great strides toward increasing civil rights and political opportunities for people of Mexican descent, and by the 1980s, Mexican Americans had achieved several of their objectives—more educational opportunities, job access, and voting rights.

One issue, however, that had divided the Mexican American community since the 1930s was illegal immigration. While many Mexican Americans saw little problem with those immigrants, others wanted to do all they could do stop illegal immigration. That division of opinion continued into the twenty-first century as the United States attempted to come to grips with the growing illegal immigration from Mexico.

CHAPTER SIX

Border Crossings and Illegal Immigration

For decades there was no such thing as illegal immigration from Mexico to the United States. Indeed, the issue of undocumented immigrants rarely arose before 1929 because the U.S. government had few restrictions on Mexican immigration. Even as the United States began in the 1930s to tighten its control of the two-thousand-mile border, efforts to stop illegal immigrants varied depending on the political climate and the condition of the U.S. economy. Moreover, American officials had long acknowledged that Mexican labor was essential to the growth of the United States and its continued prosperity.

There are only estimates of the numbers of undocumented Mexicans who cross the border to live in the United States. At times taking advantage of anti-Mexican prejudices or xenophobia, politicians and others have made wild guesses about the number of illegal Mexican immigrants in the United States. Researchers have used various surveys and demographic studies to make calculations. From 1925 to 1946 the Immigration and Naturalization Service (INS) reported finding fewer than one hundred thousand such Mexican immigrants a year. By the end of the 1970s estimates of Mexicans living illegally in the United States reached between 3 and 6 million. But the number remains elusive. The only certainties are the numbers of undocumented workers first began to increase in the late 1940s, grew in even larger numbers after the 1960s, and continued to grow into the twentieth-first century.

Whether illegal immigrants entered a country encouraging them to come or one trying to stop them seemed to matter little to those who entered the United States in hope of finding their dreams. By the late twentieth century immigrants were willing to risk their lives in order to find opportunity for themselves and their children.

The Two-Thousand-Mile Border Begins Closing

When the great first wave of Mexican immigrants began coming to the United States at the beginning of the twentieth century, there were few who worried about immigration from Mexico, and there was no Border Patrol. Federal employees known as Mounted Watchmen rode on horseback along the stretching border from San Diego, California, to Brownsville, Texas, but their job was to keep an eye out for smugglers of taxable goods such as cigarettes or alcohol. The first real immigration restrictions were

U.S. soldiers interview Mexicans wanting to emigrate to America. The U.S. government imposed few restrictions on Mexican immigration until the early twentieth century.

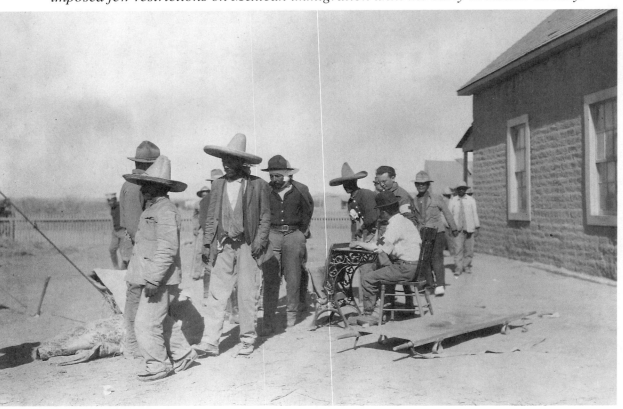

laws passed in 1917, declaring each Mexican immigrant had to pay a tax of eight-dollars and pass a literacy test in Spanish before being admitted to the United States. What then was called the Bureau of Immigration had a few stations along the border, and even at these points the tax and the test were often waived. Crossing remained easy until the end of the 1920s. Mexicans wanting to come to the United States merely walked, drove a wagon or car, rode a horse, or took a ship or a train across the border and registered whenever they wanted to become legal immigrants rather than visitors. The immigration laws of the late nineteenth century and early twentieth century were designed to limit immigrants from Asia or Europe and left Mexican immigration wide open.

In 1921 and again in 1924, the U.S. government imposed restrictions on the number of immigrants who could enter from certain countries, but these quotas did not apply to Mexicans. So all Mexican immigrants had to do to be considered legal was to register. Jesus Garza, who later laid track for the railroads, dug ditches, worked in restaurants, and performed other low-skill jobs, found it easy to come to the United States. Like so many others he went to a border town in Mexico and arrived in the United States by train. As he told of his crossing later,

When I was about twenty I decided to leave home and come here. . . . I took out [enough] money to take me to San Antonio and took the train for Nuevo Laredo. I crossed the border there. I had no trouble, although it was the first time I had come. I paid my $8.00, passed my examination, then changed my Mexican coins for American money and went to San Antonio, Texas.[54]

Restrictions on Mexican immigration tightened slightly with the passage of the 1924 Immigration Act. Under this law, Mexican immigrants now had to get a visa before entering the United States. The visa fee was ten dollars, which was in addition to the eight-dollar tax already in place. For many escaping dire poverty in Mexico, such fees proved too high a price to pay, and so many Mexican immigrants simply crossed the border without reporting to immigration officials. In 1924 Congress established a Border Patrol, whose job would be to stop immigrants without proper papers from slipping across either from Mexico or Canada. It was a small force, however, and it had few resources for patrolling the long border between the United States and Mexico.

The Bracero Program

Another policy that unintentionally encouraged illegal immigration and made controlling immigration from Mexico more difficult was the federal government's sponsoring of guest, or temporary, workers coming to the United States. The men admitted under this policy were called "braceros" from the Spanish word for arm, *brazo*. The idea was that during World War I, as American servicemen left their jobs to join the military, braceros would fill the temporary void in the

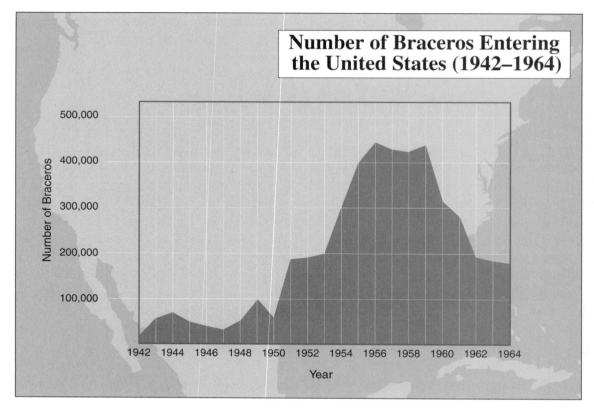

Number of Braceros Entering the United States (1942–1964)

American labor force. In 1917 Mexico and the United States agreed the workers would have transportation from recruiting stations in Mexico to the fields and orchards in the United States, decent housing, and fair wages. The braceros would be returned to Mexico after six months. Despite the return provision, many who first came as braceros under this and subsequent similar programs eventually settled in the United States and became citizens.

Workers in the bracero programs often faced abuse from their employers, and this motivated some participants to leave their temporary jobs, essentially becoming illegal immigrants. Some employers saw the workers merely as beasts of burden who would do any job, no matter how difficult, under any conditions from picking cotton under the blazing sun without water to bending over in the dusty fields, hoeing sugar beets from dawn to dark. Besides harsh working conditions, workers were often cheated out of fair wages, housed in old stables, falling-down shacks, or chicken coops, and treated worse than animals. The Reverend Leo F. Dworschak wrote in 1952 that "farmers in his area appeared to have no sense of responsibility towards braceros. . . . [I]n some instances they [the farmers] provide better care for their cattle than they do for their workers."[55]

At least one employer treated braceros as virtual slaves and even locked them up when they complained. Manuel Aguilar, working for the Mexican ministry of foreign affairs, investigated some of the complaints by Mexican workers. Aguilar said,

About twenty of the fifty-one men who had been sent to work for [a Tennessee man] . . . had skipped their

The Life of a Bracero

Ramon Gonzales was just a toddler when his parents crossed the border as illegal immigrants. He lived most of his life in the United States but returned to Mexico as a young man. Ramon wanted to go back to the United States and crossed the border illegally several times. Sometimes immigration officials caught and deported him. In *Between Two Cultures*, he describes how he decided to come to the United States with the bracero program:

I came to Mexico City because they were going to send some men to the United States as braceros . . . and there were thousands of people waiting there to get jobs as braceros. Oh, I thought, I would never get there because there were thousands. So finally one man told me, "You want to go as a bracero?" I said, "Yes." "Well, I will sell you a pass to get in." I said, "How much you want for that pass?" "Well," he said, "give me one hundred pesos [Mexican dollars]." . . . So I gave him a hundred pesos for the pass, and I got in to see the doctor for a physical check and everything. Finally . . . they told us to be in the railroad station at a certain time.

And we all got in the train; it was about six or seven cars of all braceros. I was the only one who could speak English.

And when the train came, . . . [t]hey had our papers, and everything was clear. We crossed the border, and they brought us . . . on the train, all the way to Fresno, California. . . . [T]here were a lot of ranchers. They would give, say, fifty dollars for fifty guys. And then one rancher asked, "Any of you guys speak English?" So I said, "Yes, a little." "Well, I want you to pick out fifty of the best you think are good workers." So I told him, "OK," so I picked out most of the guys that came from the town that I was born in, and we went to work for him. The rancher told me, "You're going to be my foreman." I says, "I don't like to be foreman because these men, I tell them what to do, then they get mad." "No, you're going to get better pay than they do; you be my foreman." I say OK. So he teach me how to prune trees, and then I had to tell the men how to prune the trees. And after that, when something was wrong they would tell me, "Well, you tell the boss!"

contracts as a result of inadequate housing and cooking facilities and being overcharged for food. Others had skipped after some of their colleagues [fellow laborers] had been incarcerated [jailed] by this person after they had verbally protested the poor conditions in which they were forced to live.[56]

In addition to employers who abused their braceros, there were those who obeyed other provisions of the bracero program but who would ask good workers to return on their own the next season. By operating outside the official program, the farmer was guaranteed a corps of workers who already knew how to prune the grapevines or pick fruit properly. In this way many men who had first come legally as braceros ended up working illegally in the United States.

The Dangers of the Crossing

Once a Mexican who wanted to come to the United States without papers made up his mind to do so, he had to decide where and how to cross the border. The methods and places of making a border crossing varied with the changing times. During the 1940s and 1950s, those who wished to enter the United States illegally usually hid in cars or trucks or hiked across open land, keeping a sharp eye out to avoid the Border Patrol. Others crossing into Texas waded or swam across the Rio Grande.

The relative ease of the crossing meant that many Mexicans made repeated trips across the border, living part of the year in Mexico and part of the year in the United States. Ramon Gonzales was one such migrant. He explains how he would set off with some friends, planning to reach the United States:

We never jumped the border in the day time. Every time it was in the night [you could see the lights]. . . . It is in this direction, and you cross a mountain and come to another one. We would sleep out in the bushes. You have a jacket or something, and you just lay down there in the bushes. You bring food for a certain number of days. You figure, well, it's going to take three days, so you bring enough food and water. So you sleep under a tree all day, until when it gets dark you start going again. That's how we used to do it.[57]

Although in the early days of restricted immigration Mexicans could cross with relatively little fear of getting caught by the Border Patrol, the journey north could still be risky. Historian Juan Ramon García explains:

As many unfortunate individuals discovered, the journey into the United States was fraught with natural and man-made hazards which at times turned the crossing into a nightmare, ending in severe injuries and death. Those who sought to enter illegally often faced torrid temperatures in the day and freezing weather at night. At times they could not carry sufficient food or water to make the journey. There was the ever-present danger of snakebites or of falling victim to the vicious gangs that operated along the border. Unknown numbers of braceros and undocumented workers were robbed and even killed for their meager earnings or personal possessions. Undocumented workers were shot at or beaten by local ruffians as they attempted to cut across private lands. The Rio Grande claimed its share of victims through drowning. In 1953, its swollen flood waters claimed between 300 and 400 victims who had attempted to cross it.[58]

Just how difficult a crossing might be was often hard to predict. Over the years the Border Patrol faced problems of lack of personnel needed to do its job, money to run its offices, and equipment. In addition, at various times the INS turned a blind eye to border crossings by illegal workers, and sometimes even aided undocumented workers in entering the United States. In October 1948, for example, the border agents helped commercial farms get the workers they needed to harvest ripening crops. On this occasion Mexico was slow in preparing papers for guest workers standing in Ciudad Juárez, across the river from El Paso, Texas. Trucks to the cotton fields stood by in El Paso waiting to take the workers to the fields to pick. As the cotton pickers crossed without papers, the Border Patrol arrested them and then "paroled" them to the anxious cotton growers. The buses immediately whisked the workers to the fields to begin picking the ripe cotton. After seven thousand undocumented workers had crossed; and

there were sufficient crop pickers, the INS again closed the border letting no more undocumented workers come.

Operation Wetback

Large-scale efforts to root out undocumented workers usually came when there was less need for labor, or—as happened during the 1950s—U.S. political leaders stirred up widespread concern about immigration among their constituents. In 1952 Congress passed the McCarran-Walter Immigration and Nationality Act, which restricted immigration and allowed naturalized citizens to be deported if they were involved in antigovernmental activities. Commentators in newspapers and on radios began to talk about what they called illegal hordes invading the United States and causing economic and social problems. The American public responded with cries for a tightening up of the border, and in 1954 the United States launched a hunt for undocumented aliens known as Operation Wetback.

The Immigration and Naturalization Service (INS) began a military-like campaign with squads of Border Patrol agents swooping down on apartments, fields, orchards, canning houses, and factories to round up undocumented workers. Anyone who could not provide papers was arrested. In these dragnet-style operations, American citizens of Mexican descent were often arrested if they were not carrying proof of their citizenship. Operation Wetback moved across California and the Southwest for several months, during which time American authorities deported more than 1 million immigrants. The INS finally declared victory and discontinued the operation, and in 1955, in his annual report, General Joseph M. Swing, the INS commissioner, wrote that the problem of illegal immigration had ended and the gaps in the border had been closed.

The victory declaration was premature. Although the numbers of undocumented workers shrank for a short period of time, before many years had passed thousands more had journeyed across the border. In 1969, for example, the INS took 202,000 undocumented workers into custody, and

The Immigration and Naturalization Service launched Operation Wetback in 1954 to deport large numbers of undocumented workers like these Mexicans entering the United States via the Rio Grande.

the numbers of such arrests continued to grow. Just ten years later the INS reported finding 831,000 Mexicans without papers. At the same time, changes in U.S. laws made it easier for those with special skills or with relatives living in the United States to come legally, while making immigration even more difficult for unskilled foreigners without family already in the United States. And so for many would-be immigrants from Mexico, their only option was to come without papers.

The Amnesty Act of 1986

By the 1980s, public concern over an apparent flood of undocumented workers forced government officials to take action. In 1986 Congress passed the Immigration Reform and Control Act, also known as the Amnesty Act. This bill contained four major parts to deal with illegal immigration: It provided more money for the Border Patrol to tighten control of the border; it set a number of penalties and fines for employers who knowingly hired undocumented workers; the law said guest-worker programs could continue only if there were no laborers in the United States who wanted the jobs; and it allowed many illegal immigrants who had been living in the United States the opportunity to become permanent legal residents and eventually apply for citizenship. The last provision greatly impacted the Mexican American community. All undocumented immigrants needed to do was prove they had lived in the United States since at least 1983 and had worked in agriculture for at least ninety days dur-

ing the three years from 1983 to 1986. Under the Amnesty Act about 1.8 million Mexicans applied for amnesty and became legal residents.

Although the Amnesty Act was designed to stop illegal Mexican immigration, it failed to accomplish that. The law required employers to check the documents of their workers, but employers had few means of verifying the authenticity of those papers. All a worker living in the United States illegally had to do was obtain forged documents—something that was easily done.

Avoiding *la Migra*

Mexicans and others desperate for work continue to come across the border. Still, for those who manage to elude the Border Patrol, make it safely to the United States, and find a job, life is uncertain. Always they have to be on the lookout for *la migra*, as the immigration officers are known. INS agents might search for undocumented workers at the places where they work. Restaurants, farm fields, canneries, construction sites, or meatpacking plants sometimes receive visits from officials looking for illegal immigrants. Camelia Palafox first came across the border from Tijuana, Mexico, to San Diego with forged documents. She went to work as a waitress in a Mexican-food restaurant, but she lived in fear of the *la migra*, because she knew her papers would not withstand close examination. She remembers,

> Every once in a while *la migra* would
> arrest a bus load of undocumented

people. Sometimes they would go under cover and check out the scene. Next thing you knew people were running all over the place. I was lucky because most of the time when they came, I was either off work or was on the way there. I think it was pure luck I didn't get apprehended by the INS like some of my co-workers.

I felt ashamed that I didn't have papers. I felt inferior. . . . I thought that if people found out that I didn't speak English, that they would know I didn't have papers. I was scared that I would get put in a van with other people. I felt like we would get treated like animals, as if we were the dogs and they [INS] were the dog catchers.[59]

From Illegal Immigrant to U.S. Citizen

Camelia Palafox was one of seventeen children and as a little girl she longed to be a singer. When she grew up she decided she wanted to have a better life for her son in the United States. She crossed the border illegally and started cleaning houses in San Diego, California. Camelia Palafox's son José recorded her story for a college project, and historian Ronald Takaki included it in his book, *A Larger Memory.*

Camelia worked hard in San Diego and soon got a better paying job in a Mexican restaurant. The owners of the restaurant helped out new arrivals, and gave Camelia work. Still she told her son how afraid she was at first of getting caught:

"Even just to go to the store, I was scared to ask for stuff. Instead, I would ask somebody else to ask for me. . . . I don't know, maybe I thought the INS was everywhere

because I looked out for them a lot. Still, I think that even if one is undocumented, they should have rights and not have to be scared all the time. It shouldn't matter if one is legal or illegal, in the end they are human beings and should be treated as such."

Later she became a citizen. "Now that I'm a U.S. citizen, I feel little safer. . . . One can vote and have their voice be heard. . . . I'm proud that I've never had to get handouts from the government. I'm glad I never had to get on welfare or anything like that." And she is proud of her children. "I don't regret anything, I just feel like I'm getting old and I want to experience other things in life besides work and work. I have faith that things will be better. One has to always have hopes, or else they won't get anything done."

Rosa Crosses the Border

In his book *Crossing Over* journalist Rubén Martínez describes the difficult journey of an illegal immigrant. Rosa Chávez lived in Cherán, Mexico, a poor village where the men often traveled to the United States to work. Her husband, Wense, found a job in St. Louis, Missouri, and wanted Rosa and their two-year-old daughter Yeni to join him. It was a difficult decision, but Rosa was determined to find a better life for her daughter. Rosa paid a thousand dollars to a "coyote," Mr. Charlie, to take her and Yeni across the border.

On December 27, 1996, Rosa, Yeni, and seventeen other women, two men, and four other children left the village. They rode a bus for thirty-eight hours before reaching the border town of Nogales. The group made four attempts to cross the border, each time they were captured and returned by the *migra* (immigration officers). One night,

> They hiked in rugged terrain. . . . Crawling underneath a barbed-wire fence, Rosa got her *rebozo* [shawl] caught in the rusty metal and Yeni scratched her leg badly.

> This time they walked for six hours. . . . It was a brutally cold night. They passed through ranch land where cows and horses slept. . . .

> But the terrain only grew more rugged. Rosa lost her footing . . . and [fell], tearing open both her jeans and skin. [Yet she held Yeni tight and] the child wasn't hurt. Rosa felt blood trickling down her calf. . . . She willed herself to take one step after another, her body feeling terribly heavy and slow. . . . The rest of the way she held on to the coyote's coat, using it as a walking stick.

> Soon her thirst was unbearable. . . . Rosa's mouth was cold and dry, her face burning and wet with sweat.

> The van picked them up at the appointed spot. The *migra* were nowhere in sight.

In the United States now, Rosa and Yeni still had a thousand miles left to go. They packed into another van, traveling two more weeks through the snow and cold of a Midwestern winter before Rosa and Yeni finally reached Wense, safely.

Border Patrol agents enforce the laws. For those caught by the INS, the result is usually an arrest. These undocumented immigrants would normally be taken to a detention center, questioned, and then deported to Mexico. Rosa Chavez, who made several attempts to cross the border from Mexico, told a reporter about the first time she got caught and was detained by the Border Patrol as she attempted, along with several others who also had no papers, to cross the border illegally. First they walked across the border and then met a van on a rural road. Reporter Rubén Martínez explains,

> They'd driven only about fifteen minutes when a police squad car pulled them over. They sat by the edge of the road until several Border Patrol units took them back to BP headquarters. Rosa was scared; this was the first time she'd been detained by the *migra* and she didn't know what to expect. The interrogation lasted all of a minute. Name, date of birth, home address in Mexico. They took her fingerprints on a digital pad. Every time the American agent spoke, all she heard was the strange accent with which he pronounced the words in Spanish. Soon she was laughing in the middle of her responses, relaxed, a bit giddy even.[60]

Although those illegal immigrants who manage to get into the country are still subject to arrest and deportation, with too few INS officers and too many undocumented workers, the Border Patrol has used "voluntary" departure for those caught in the country unlawfully. In what they call sanctions work, the agents might find out there are illegal workers employed in a particular business, and then they call the employer and warn them about the undocumented immigrants. The employer is required to fire the illegal workers or pay

a fine. But as INS agent-in-charge in New Mexico, Charles Kirk explains,

> With 12 agents covering New Mexico, the INS doesn't have the resources to detain and deport in all situations. . . .

> When the INS is conducting sanctions work—where agents investigate claims that undocumented workers are employed in the country—they only are required to report the illegal residents they find to their employers. If these workers are not fired, employers could face a fine of up to $3,000 per person.

> The law states that we have to tell the company [we don't have to go catch immigrants]. Should we come in contact with them [the undocumented workers], yes we would have to arrest them . . . . We realize they're probably just going to go find another job.

> [But] during busy times, we don't even get a chance to do sanctions work.[61]

Other Operations

By the end of the 1990s illegal crossings had grown back to their 1980s levels. New operations were designed to tighten control of the lengthy border as well as to round up those already working in the United States without legal papers. In 1993 the government launched Operation Hold the Line between Ciudad Juárez,

Mexico, and El Paso, Texas. With an enormous show of personnel and vehicles along the border, the Border Patrol was able to slow the influx of immigrants by about 73 percent. But while there was a decrease in illegal crossings at El Paso, there was an increase at other less populated places along the border. Similarly, in 1994 as part of Operation Gatekeeper, the United States built massive steel walls and even taller fences topped with barbed wire along the border near San Diego, California; Nogales, Arizona; and El Paso, Texas, but such barriers failed to stop those who wanted to reach the United States. They found those long stretches of desert or wilderness that remained lightly patrolled.

Tightening border security, however, forces Mexicans wanting to come to the United States without proper papers to employ the services of guides known as "coyotes." For a fee, the coyote promises to guide them safely into the United States. By the end of the twentieth century these coyotes were often part of big smuggling rings. They charge high fees, allowing poor immigrants to make a deposit with final payments due after they get a job in the United States. According to Santiago Creel, interior minister of Mexico, "the Mexican government has identified more than 100 people smuggling networks charging between $1,500 and $8,000 per person."[62]

With or without the services of a coyote, the crossings have grown more perilous with the passing years as the INS tightens up its watch of the international boundary. Crossing as far as possible from the border towns, immigrants trek across miles of arid wilderness or through the mountains. By the end of the twentieth

Death Along the Border

On May 18, 2003, in Houston, Texas, a crowd of about four hundred mourners assembled to observe a memorial mass for the nineteen men, women, and children who had died trying to cross the U.S.-Mexican border. Those dead were part of a group of sixty-eight people, young and old, who had been told they would be transported to the United States in an air-conditioned truck. Instead, they were packed into an eighteen-wheel trailer truck with closed doors that could not be opened from the inside, where temperatures rose above one hundred degrees. They ended up traveling in a moving oven.

Some escaped the ordeal with their lives, but when the truck driver realized some of his passengers were dying, he abandoned the truck. Law enforcement officials and INS have failed to discover his identity.

Such tragedies are common in the desert regions of the United States. In southern Texas, it is well known that during the summer months when the temperatures climb, the death rates among illegal immigrants will climb also.

century, thousands of men, women, and children had lost their lives trying to cross the border. Some suffocated inside trucks or died of heat in temperatures over one hundred degrees. Others, hiking through the mountains in wintertime, froze to death. Death from thirst awaited many who tried desert crossings. Some, stuffed into cars or vans, suffered fatal crashes in attempts to escape pursuing Border Patrol agents.

According to Interior minister Creel, "About 1,000 people a day take the risk often guided by unscrupulous smugglers ready to abandon them at the first sign of trouble. Last year [2002] about 371 bodies were recovered along the 2,000-mile Mexican-U.S. border."[63]

Despite all the dangers and all the measures to keep undocumented workers out, many Mexicans living in poverty long to better their lives and those of their children. They are willing to face grave dangers in order to fulfill their dreams. They are willing to work hard as undocumented workers have in the past, and they are willing to risk all for a chance at the American dream.

CHAPTER SEVEN

Living the American Dream

While policies toward undocumented workers grow stricter, Mexican Americans and their children find more opportunities than ever in the United States. By the 1980s, many of the civil rights fought for by Chicano activists had been won. Thanks to constant pressure to improve schools serving Mexican Americans, more than 80 percent of second-generation Mexican Americans graduated from high school. As immigrants' children settled into mainstream life, they found most doors open to them. Mexican Americans also shared in the country's prosperity, as many reached the middle class and beyond.

The Business World

Because of their new buying power and increasing numbers, some in the business world called the 1980s "The Decade of the Hispanic." Anglo-owned businesses are profiting from the prosperity among Mexican Americans, but by the beginning of the twenty-first century Mexican Americans owned businesses in all fifty states, many with incomes in the millions. Hispanic-owned businesses grew by 321 percent between the 1970s and 1990s, and of these Mexican Americans owned more than half.

Often, these businesses catered to the growing desire of Anglos to experience some aspect of Mexican American culture. Mexican American and immigrant entrepreneurs filled this demand from New York to Hawaii. Immigrants living in the barrios had long served up foods such as tacos, enchiladas, tamales, or refried beans for other Mexican Americans, and Anglos began to patronize these establishments. At other times, Anglos went to the barrios looking for items such as piñatas, Mexican style clay pots, or wood-carvings for their home or garden. Before long many of these businesses expanded beyond the barrios.

Fernando Sanchez, fondly called *el Gordo* (the Fat One), is an example of a man who moved from fulfilling the needs of barrio residents to selling to a multi-ethnic clientele.

Sanchez worked for years in restaurants and factories in New York City before he opened a tortilla shop (*tortilleria*). His business grew as he produced more and more tortillas and sold them to customers

As Anglo interest in Mexican culture increased, Mexican Americans like this restaurant owner saw their businesses prosper.

farther and farther from the city. Within ten years he owned six trucks, several *tortillerias*, and employed over fifty people. Eventually, annual sales reached about $4 million. As Sanchez built his operation, like other successful Mexican Americans, he helped some of his workers start their own businesses.

Mexican American Literary Traditions

The growing presence of Mexican Americans in the economic mainstream of the United States has been matched by their increasing impact on the literary and artistic scene. The Chicano movement inspired an outpouring of books, plays, artworks, and films in which Mexican Americans portrayed their lifestyles, communities, and concerns. At first these artists appealed only to Chicanos or other Spanish speakers. But Chicanos soon discovered audiences beyond the Mexican American community.

Sometimes, Mexican Americans drew on their traditions to produce works that carried powerful political messages. For example, Cesar Chavez, the labor leader, remembered his mother, Juana, trying to teach her young children to behave using *cuentos* (Mexican folktales often told to children) and *dichos* (moral sayings and proverbs). Chavez recalled how she would remind him, "He who never listens to advice will never grow to be old." One story she repeated often "[was the] story of the stone freezing in the boy's hand . . . a very disobedient son who came home drunk and got real mad at his mother. He picked up a rock and was about to throw it at her when it froze to his hand."[64]

Chavez, recalling the power simple tales like this could have, called upon Luis Valdez, a young Mexican American playwright and activist, to write skits in Spanish to help convey the UFW's message to potential members. In response, in 1965 Valdez founded El Teatro Campesino (The Farm Workers Theater). The farmworkers loved his skits, but he was so successful in using Mexican legends, symbols, and a variety of theater traditions that his works won a wider following. Valdez inspired and trained a whole new group of artists who started other *teatros* to present information or political messages in humorous plays in Spanish. The *teatros* later drew diverse audiences and some of the plays won international acclaim.

Mexican American women playwrights also gained a following among theatergoers in the years following the Chicano movement. For example, Estela Portillo Trambley in her play, *The Day of the Swallows*, broke new ground with her main character Doña Josefa, who looks from a female perspective at the Mexican American tradition of male dominance. Because it also addresses issues that affect women in general, Portillo Trambley's work helped bring Mexican American theater to the attention of Anglo audiences.

Just as playwrights found success, Mexican American writers found wide audiences for novels that convey their ethnic perspective; for example, José Antonio Villarreal's 1959 novel *Pocho*, about the conflict a young Mexican American experiences

Labor leader Cesar Chavez (left) stands beside playwright Luis Valdez. Valdez began creating skits for United Farm Workers members and went on to write for popular theater.

between his family and mainstream culture. Villarreal's novel found few readers, but as awareness of Chicano culture expanded, many other Mexican American artists attracted notice among Anglo critics. Tomás Rivera wrote a prize-winning novel of a young migrant's struggles with discrimination, titled *And the Earth Did not Part*. In 1972 Rudolfo Anaya wrote *Bless Me, Ultima*, which conveys a sense of the richness of Mexican American culture through the story of a young Mexican American growing up in New Mexico.

Besides being accepted by a broader readership in the United States, works by Mexican American authors have won both national and international prizes for literature. Ana Castillo, for example, won an American Book Award for her first novel *The Mixquiahuala Letters*, which includes Mexican Americans as main characters. Another award-winning author, Sandra Cisneros, describes life in an ethnic neighborhood of Chicago in the best seller, *The House on Mango Street*.

Today books for both adults and young people describe the lives of Mexican Americans, and the continued popularity of these ethnic novels is one measure of how the literary world has embraced the works of Chicano writers. For young people, *The Circuit* by Francisco Jiménez and its sequel, *Breaking Through*, tell of a migrant child whose family is eventually caught by the INS. In the *Parrot in the Oven*, by Victor Martinez, a Chicano teenager faces the challenge of growing up in poverty in a small California town. Gary Soto, author of several books and poems, wrote *Jess* the story of two young Mexican American brothers trying to escape farm labor and get a college education.

On the Screen and Stage

No longer outsiders in the American cultural mainstream, by the 1980s Mexican Americans had also made a noticeable impact on the movie and TV industry as works reflecting Mexican American traditions and lives appeared on the screen. The first film to feature Chicanos and their experiences and to attract large audiences was *La Bamba*, written and directed by Luis Valdez. It is based on the life of 1950s Mexican American pop star Ritchie Valens.

With the production of plays and movies about Mexican Americans lives, Chicano actors and actresses found increasing opportunities for starring roles. Moreover, these new roles went beyond those that had long fostered negative stereotypes of Mexican Americans. Up

Actor Edward James Olmos (left) demonstrates a calculus model in a scene from Stand and Deliver. *Olmos received an Academy Award nomination for his work in that film.*

until the 1980s, the experience of Mexican American actress Lupe Ontiveros had been typical. Beginning in the 1970s, Ontiveros played in almost 200 movies and later in TV sitcoms. By her estimate, in at least 150 of these appearances she played a maid. She told an interviewer, "It's their [Hollywood's] perspective of who we are. They don't know we're very much a part of this country and that we make up every part of this country." Although she is a college graduate and the daughter of immigrants who owned restaurants and tortilla factories, she believes she must still use an accent to get parts. "When I go in there and speak perfect English, I don't get the part,"[65] she says.

But such stereotyping mostly ended by the end of the twentieth century. Ruth Livier's experience exemplifies how the roles available to Mexican Americans have broadened. Unlike the typecasting that Lupe Ontiveros experienced, Livier finds herself cast in diverse roles. Other Mexican Americans, such as Edward James Olmos, have became familiar faces on the stage and screen although they still often portray Mexican Americans. Olmos was nominated for the prestigious Tony Award and won the Los Angeles Drama Critics Circle Award for his portrayal of El Pachuco in Luis Valdez's play *Zoot Suit*. In 1987 Olmos was nominated for an Academy Award for his role as the barrio teacher Jaime Escalante, in the movie *Stand and Deliver*. From there Olmos went on to play many other characters in movies and on TV. Later, Olmos established his own production company to produce Latino films, which found mainstream audiences.

Murals and the Visual Arts

Just as with literature and the performing arts, the Chicano movement helped bring Mexican American visual art traditions to the attention of a wider audience. Inspired by renowned Mexican muralists Diego Rivera, David Alfaro Siqueiros, and José Clemente Orozco, Chicano artists used bridges, fences, freeway overpasses, or any available outdoor space on which to produce their murals. Commissions by private foundations and government entities helped foster this art form across the country, and murals by artists such as Susan Cervantes and John Valadez can be seen in cities from New York to San Francisco.

Mexican American artists draw on the mural tradition in producing large works on canvas as well. John Valadez and Carlos Almaraz have created murals and other arts works for the U.S. and international markets.

Just as the murals of Diego Rivera convey political themes and celebrate the working class, Luiz Jiménez creates sculptures incorporating themes of the working-class Chicano community. His work appears in museums such as the National Gallery in Washington, D.C., and the Museum of Modern Art and the Metropolitan Museum in New York City. Carmen Lomas Garza is an artist who uses girlhood memories of everyday activities, such as making tamales, to create oil paintings, gouache works, or lithographs.

The Mural Tradition Lives On with John Valadez

John Valadez was a teenager growing up in East Los Angeles when the Chicano movement brought changes to the lives of Mexican Americans. It was the visual arts, especially Chicano murals, that helped to change the way Americans viewed Mexican Americans and helped to change the American art world.

Valadez attended East Los Angeles College in the early 1970s and went on to California State University at Long Beach to earn a bachelor of fine arts degree in 1976. He designed and worked on several mural projects with young people. He painted murals for commissions and collaborated with another Mexican American muralist, Carlos Almaraz on *Return of the Maya* in 1979.

In 1981, after five years taking photographs of street scenes along Broadway in New York, Valadez completed *The Broadway Mural* for the Victor Clothing Company at 240 South Broadway, between Second and Third Streets. The eight-by-sixty-foot canvas hangs inside on the first floor. Ten years later he completed a mural for the General Services Administration in El Paso, Texas. From 1996–1998 he worked on *We The People: Summer Festivals of Orange County* for the federal courthouse in Santa Ana, California. Another mural *The Top Hat Bridal Shop Mural* appears in New York and shows four brides in varying wedding scenes.

Besides murals Valadez works with pastels and lithographs and has exhibited his art in galleries from San Francisco to New York. He is only one of the nationally and internationally known Mexican American artists whose creations have found recognition in the visual arts world since the Chicano movement.

Lomas Garza has exhibited her work in museums all over the United States, including the Hirshhorn Museum and Sculpture Garden of the Smithsonian Institution in Washington, D. C., the San José Museum of Art and the Oakland Museum in California, and the Whitney Museum of American Art in New York City. These artists, among others, demonstrate how Mexican American artists have gained acceptance by not only the national but worldwide artistic mainstream.

Music Old and New

While wide acceptance in the visual arts generally came after the advent of the Chicano movement, the music world accepted Mexican American musicians even earlier. The breakthrough into American popular music for modern-day Mexican American recording artists came in the 1950s when Ritchie Valens changed the American music scene by becoming a rock and roll star. Drawing on Mexican folk tunes and popular music, he recorded

"La Bamba," "Donna," and "Come On, Let's Go," all of which became hits.

Ritchie Valens's success changed the minds of the record industry executives, who had previously believed that Anglos would never listen to songs in Spanish. As a result, by the beginning of the twenty-first century, many artists recorded in both languages. Linda Ronstadt, born in Tucson, Arizona, to Mexican American parents, demonstrates the broad audience appeal of Mexican Americans. Ronstadt sings using styles from mariachi to country to operetta and continues to be popular among both English and Spanish speakers. Carlos Santana's band began in the 1960s using Latin jazz and rock sounds and his music similarly caught on with Anglo audiences. Santana's popularity reaches into the twenty-first century—in 2000 he received Grammy awards for best recording in nine different categories.

Santana and Valens before him drew on a long Mexican American musical tradition. These artists combined older styles with American pop music to find success, and their works evoke the *corridos*—folk ballads—that tell of love lost, great historical events, tales of bravery, or important moments in a person's life. Mexican-origin people often wrote *corridos* to tell of their life experiences such as leaving Mexico for the United States, going off to fight in World War II, struggling to find a place in the United States, or the pain of losing a sweetheart.

Akin to the *corridos* are the *rancheras*—like American country western songs—which remain popular among Mexican Americans. Frances Esquibel Ty-woniak remembers how, when she was a young child in New Mexico, people gathered to relax and sing: "My father played the guitar, and often, after work or on weekends, he would sit around with the other men who helped on the ranch or who worked on nearby ranches, and sing Mexican ranch songs—*rancheras*. My father knew these songs from Mexico and from his work experience in Texas."[66]

While *rancheras* have large radio audiences today, an entirely new form of music was born in Texas. Known as *conjunto*, Mexican immigrants in South Texas created music with guitars and with the accordions the German immigrant population brought to the state. *Conjunto*, like blues and jazz, is a uniquely American style of music, although it has developed a following in Europe as well as the United States.

Making It in Sports

From the music scene to literature to the performing arts to the sports world, Mexican Americans had established a place for themselves in American society by the end of the twentieth century. But unlike other arenas, almost from the beginning Mexican American athletes found acceptance in the sports mainstream. In 1882, for example, Californian Vincent Nava became the first Mexican American major league baseball player as a catcher for the Providence Grays and later the Baltimore Orioles. In the 1930s Lefty Gomez achieved lasting fame pitching for the New York Yankees. Gomez's 189 wins resulted in his being inducted into the Baseball Hall of Fame in 1972. At the beginning of the twenty-first century such stars as Nomar Garciaparra, shortstop for the Boston Red Sox, continue the great Mexican American baseball tradition. Garciaparra is only the third Red Sox player to hit homers twice in one inning. He was one of the American League's top ten batting champions in 1999 and continues to make winning plays for his team.

In football, too, talented athletes of Mexican heritage have achieved wide acclaim. Jim Plunkett, playing as a quarterback for Stanford University, was the 1970 Heisman Trophy winner. Plunkett went on to star for the Oakland Raiders, staying in the NFL for seventeen years and appearing in two Super Bowls. Anthony Muñoz, whose grandparents emigrated from Chihuahua, Mexico, first played college football for the University of Southern California where he won the Lombardi Trophy, which is awarded every year to the top college lineman. Muñoz had a successful career with the Cincinnati Bengals, going with his team to two

Boston Red Sox shortstop Nomar Garciaparra hits a home run in a 1998 game. Garciaparra is one of many successful Mexican American athletes.

American Football Conference Championships and being elected to play in eleven consecutive Pro Bowls. In 1998 he was named to the Pro Football Hall of Fame, the first Latino to be so honored. In 1999 he also received the Hispanic Heritage Award for great achievement in sports.

Science, Medicine, and the Nobel Prize

In addition to arts and entertainment, Mexican Americans have had an enormous impact in the sciences. Two Mexican Americans have been honored with the most prestigious award for scientists—the Nobel Prize in physics and chemistry, respectively. Luis Walter Alvarez was the first American of Mexican ancestry to receive the honor. Considered a pioneer in his discipline, Alvarez won the 1967 Nobel Prize in physics for his discovery of previously unknown properties of atomic nuclei. The other Nobel laureate was Mario J. Molina. Although Molina was born in Mexico City in 1943, he later emigrated to the United States. Molina attended the University of California at Berkeley and graduated with a Ph.D. in 1972. He then worked as a professor and researcher at the University of California at Irvine. Along with scientists at Berkeley and at Irvine, he discovered the mechanism by which chlorofluorocarbons, CFCs, destroy the earth's protective ozone layer. This important discovery led to the Nobel Prize. About his work Molina said, "When I first chose the project to investigate the fate of chlorofluorocarbons . . . it was simply out of scientific curiosity. I did not consider . . . the environmental consequences."[67]

Mexican Americans have made contributions to science and medicine as chemists, physicists, biologists, medical doctors, engineers, computer scientists, and even astronauts. Ellen Ochoa, who has a Ph.D. in electrical engineering, not only received three patents for her discoveries, but she also served the National Aeronautics and Space Administration (NASA) as an astronaut, making three trips into orbit aboard the space shuttle.

Spanish and Latino Media

The Mexican Americans have accomplished much in a variety of fields, and their contributions to mainstream culture are outstanding. Yet some Mexican Americans have found success by serving the specific needs of the Latino community. As early as the nineteenth century, Spanish-language newspapers kept readers who were not fluent in English informed. In addition Mexican American novelists and poets used these early newspapers to publish their work. Even though Mexican Americans became increasingly bilingual, by the twentieth century, these periodicals had expanded their coverage of issues and events of interest to the Spanish-speaking community. *La Prensa* began publishing in San Antonio in 1913, and was established by Ignacio E. Lorenzo, who also started *La Opinión* in Los Angeles in 1926. By 1930 *La Opinión* had a circulation of over twenty-five thousand. Still operat-

The First Mexican American Woman in Space: Ellen Ochoa

Many kids dream of becoming an astronaut, but Ellen Ochoa felt uncertain about what she wanted to do. Born in Los Angeles, California, on May 10, 1958, she had many dreams. She liked music and played the flute. She liked to write and thought about becoming a journalist. But she also liked computers. The choices seemed difficult.

Growing up, however, Ochoa knew she had to study hard, for her mother always told her how important it was to get a good education. During junior high school, her parents divorced, and she and her sister and three brothers moved to La Mesa, California, with her mother. She graduated from high school at the head of her class and went on to San Diego State University.

With all her interests, she was still unsure about her career. In college she changed her major five times before deciding on physics. By 1980, when she graduated, she knew she wanted to be an engineer. Ochoa went on to Stanford University for a master's degree and Ph.D. in electrical engineering.

In 1985 she went to work as a research engineer at Sandia National Laboratories in Livermore, California. She worked on studies of vision and light in a field known as optics. For her discoveries in optics she was granted three patents. Ochoa thought about being an astronaut and applied to the program at the National Aeronautics and Space Administration (NASA). In 1987 she began working for NASA as a research scientist, but in 1990 she was chosen for NASA's space shuttle program.

Going up in the space shuttle *Discovery* in 1993, Ochoa became the first Mexican American to travel in space. She and the crew spent nine days in space, circling the earth 148 times. They researched the earth's atmosphere. For one of the experiments, Ochoa operated a fifty-foot robot arm, sending a satellite into space. The next day Ochoa was beamed into TV sets around the world as the robot caught the satellite and Ochoa returned it to the cargo bay.

Since that first shuttle mission, Ochoa has been on two more, logging more than 719 hours in space. She continues to work as a scientist and to work with schools and teachers.

ing in the early twenty-first century, *La Opinión* and *La Prensa* continue to cover issues important to the Mexican American community.

Although these presses began by fulfilling the needs of Mexican Americans for information and entertainment in their native language, today they attract other

Spanish speakers living in the United States. Spanish-language media has grown from newspapers and journals to radio, television, and even the Internet.

The Hispanic Broadcasting Corporation (HBC) was the largest Spanish-language broadcaster and included productions from Univision, Telefura, and Galavision. Given the growth of the Mexican American and wider Latino community, the mainstream Anglo media are attempting to appeal to this large audience. For example, Telemundo, a part of the NBC Television Network, now broadcasts across the country in Spanish. From Saturday morning cartoons to afternoon soap operas, programs in Spanish Telemundo serve a broad audience of Mexican Americans and other Latinos.

A Lasting Print upon the Land

From business to the arts to sports and the sciences, Mexican Americans and their descendants have made enormous contributions to the development of America's prosperity and cultural life. Sometimes those contributions are so central to everyday existence that they are taken for granted. Still those Mexican American immigrants, who valued and maintained their unique traditions, have infused American culture with much vitality. The dauntless labor of Mexican Americans, their love of music, delight in beauty and art, appreciation of stories and tales, and their commitment to their vibrant cultural traditions have left a permanent print upon the American cultural landscape.

A Blending of Cultural Traditions

One Mexican American tradition that has found its way into American popular culture is the piñata. In Mexico piñatas were often part of the Christmas parties from December 16 to December 24. When families and friends gathered to celebrate with food, drink, and music, they usually hung a piñata for the children. The piñata was made from a clay jar, decorated with colorful paper to look like a star, a sheep, a bird, or sometimes even the Christ child's cradle. Before hanging the piñata upon a rope or string, it was filled with fruit, candy, or small toys.

When the time came, the children gathered under the decorated figure and took turns being blindfolded. With a short stick in one hand, each child was spun around before trying to hit the piñata and break it open. When someone finally succeeded, the wonderful treats fell to the ground, and shouts of delight sounded as the children hurried to pick them up.

Today colorful and variously shaped paper piñatas are used for many occasions besides Christmas celebrations. Any party, especially a birthday, provides a good opportunity to practice this old Mexican American tradition.

Just Americans

At the beginning of the twenty-first century Mexican Americans are viewed as an integral part of U.S. society, and they want to be individuals who are just Americans. Historian Oscar J. Martinez reflects on his family's experiences as being typical of Mexican Americans. Martinez grew up as the son of an undocumented worker, and his comments serve to highlight both how Mexican Americans have achieved the American dream and how some have yet to find it:

> Despite these antecedents my siblings and I managed to break the cycle of chronic marginality and enter the middle class in the United States. We were fortunate to reach young adulthood precisely at a time of increased opportunity. Three of us earned university degrees (including two Ph.D.s) and became professionals. . . . Other relatives of mine, however, have had different experiences. They have not been as fortunate on the education and employment fronts and their circumstances remain modest. The history of my extended family, I believe, mirrors what has happened to Mexican-origin people on a grander scale. Some of us, whether because of luck, greater access to good schools and good jobs, support of others, individual effort, and whatever else, have been able to better our circumstances. But many others have not.[68]

NOTES

Chapter One: Life in Mexico

1. Quoted in Robert R. Alvarez, *Familia.* Berkeley: University of California Press, 1987, p. 62.
2. Quoted in Manuel Gamio, *Mexican Immigrant: His Life Story.* New York: Arno Press and *New York Times*, 1969, p. 92.
3. Quoted in Jonathan Kandell, *La Capital.* New York: Henry Holt, 1988, p. 398.
4. Quoted in Kandell, *La Capital*, p. 399.
5. Ernesto Galarza, *Barrio Boy.* Notre Dame, IN: University of Notre Dame Press, 1971, p. 99.
6. Quoted in Marilyn P. Davis, *Mexican Voices/American Dreams.* New York: Henry Holt, 1990, pp. 9–10.
7. Quoted in Gamio, *Mexican Immigrant*, p. 9.

Chapter Two: Working in *el Norte* (the North)

8. Quoted in Oscar J. Martinez, *Mexican-Origin People in the United States.* Tucson: University of Arizona Press, 2001, p. 107.
9. Quoted in Martinez, *Mexican-Origin People in the United States*, p. 107.
10. Richard E. Lingenfelter, *The Hard Rock Miners.* Berkeley: University of California Press, 1974, p.17.
11. Quoted in Davis, *Mexican Voices/ American Dreams*, pp. 213–214.

12. Elva Treviño Hart, *Barefoot Heart.* Tempe, AZ: Bilingual Press, 1999, pp. 123, 126–127.
13. Quoted in Zaragosa Vargas, *Proletarians of the North.* Los Angeles: University of California Press, 1993, p. 88.
14. Quoted in Martinez, *Mexican-Origin People in the United States*, p. 116.

Chapter Three: Communities in Transition

15. Quoted in Martinez, *Mexican-Origin People in the United States*, p. 75.
16. Quoted in Arnoldo De León, *They Called Them Greasers.* Austin: University of Texas Press, 1983, pp. 27–28.
17. Quoted in De León, *They Called Them Greasers*, p. 28.
18. Quoted in Francisco E. Balderrama and Raymond Rodríguez, *Decade of Betrayal.* Albuquerque: University of New Mexico Press, 1995, p. 124.
19. Quoted in Shirley Anchor, *Mexican Americans in a Dallas Barrio.* Tucson: University of Arizona Press, 1979, p. 23.
20. Anchor, *Mexican Americans in a Dallas Barrio*, p. 21.
21. Treviño Hart, *Barefoot Heart*, p.105.
22. Quoted in Sarah Deutsch, *No Separate Refuge.* New York: Oxford University Press, 1987, p. 44.
23. Frances Esquibel Tywoniak and Mario T. García, *Migrant Daughter.* Berkeley: University of California Press, 2000, pp. 19–20.

24. Esquibel Tywoniak and García, *Migrant Daughter*, p. 55.
25. Galarza, *Barrio Boy*, pp. 256–57.
26. Richard Rodriguez, *Hunger of Memory*. Boston: Bantam, 1983, pp. 21–22, 41.
27. Dionicio Morales, *Dionicio Morales: A Life in Two Cultures*. Houston, TX: University of Houston, 1997, p. 105.
28. Quoted in John C. Hammerback and Richard J. Jensen, *The Rhetorical Career of Cesar Chavez*. College Station: Texas A&M University Press, 1998, p. 14.
29. Esquibel Tywoniak and García, *Migrant Daughter*, pp. 42, 48.
30. Quoted in Deutsch, *No Separate Refuge*, p. 189.

Chapter Four: Changing Times
31. Morales, *Dionicio Morales*, pp. 101–102.
32. Quoted in Mario T. García, *Mexican Americans*, New Haven, CT: Yale University Press, 1989, p.31.
33. Quoted in George J. Sánchez, *Becoming Mexican American: Ethnicity, Culture, and Identity in Chicano Los Angeles, 1900–1945*. Oxford: Oxford University Press, 1993, p. 257.
34. Quoted in Ronald Takaki, *Double Victory*. Boston: Little Brown, 2000, p. 83.
35. Raul Morin, *Among the Valiant*. Alhambra, CA: Borden, 1966, pp. 112, 114.
36. Quoted in Takaki, *Double Victory*, p. 96.
37. Quoted in Takaki, *Double Victory*, p. 98.
38. Quoted in Takaki, *Double Victory*, p. 98.
39. Quoted in Takaki, *Double Victory*, p. 84.
40. Morin, *Among the Valiant*, p.100.
41. Morin, *Among the Valiant*, pp. 277–78.
42. Quoted in Barbara Bloom, "Cesar Chavez: His Fight for the Farm Workers," *Cobblestone*, vol. 10, no. 4, April 1989, p. 34.
43. Quoted in Bloom, "Cesar Chavez," p. 35.

Chapter Five: The Chicano Movement
44. Quoted in Grace C. Huerta and Leslie A. Flemmer, "Latina Women Speak," *Social Education*, vol. 15, no. 5, September 2001, p. 273.
45. Quoted in Galán Incorporated Television & Film, "Chicano!" press review, March 26, 2003, p. 2. www.galan-inc.com.
46. Dial Torgerson, "Brown Power Unity Seen Behind School Disorders," *Los Angeles Times*, March 17, 1968.
47. Quoted in Carlos Muñoz Jr., *Youth, Identity, Power*. New York: Verso, 1989, p. 67.
48. Quoted in Muñoz, *Youth, Identity, Power*, p. 76.
49. Quoted in Richard Griswold del Castillo and Arnoldo De León, *North to Aztlán*. New York: Twayne, 1996, p. 131.
50. Quoted in Jay Mathews, "Los Angeles' New Councilwoman Reflects Changing Ethnic Politics," *Washington Post*, April 14, 1987, pp. A4+.
51. Quoted in Mathews, "Los Angeles' New Councilwoman Reflects Changing Ethnic Politics," pp. A4+.
52. Quoted in Seth Mydans, "Woman In the News: Gloria Molina," *New York Times*, February 21, 1991, pp. A17+.

53. Quoted in Davis, *Mexican Voices/ American Dreams*, p. 383.

Chapter Six: Border Crossings and Illegal Immigration

54. Quoted in Gamio, *Mexican Immigrant*, p. 15.
55. Quoted in Juan Ramon García, *Operation Wetback.* Westport, CT: Greenwood, 1980, pp. 48–49.
56. Quoted in Juan Ramon García, *Operation Wetback*, p. 47.
57. Ramon Gonzales, *Between Two Cultures.* Tucson: University of Arizona Press, 1973, p. 10.
58. García, *Operation Wetback*, p. 13.
59. Quoted in Ronald Takaki, *A Larger Memor: A History of Our Diversity with Voices.* Boston: Little Brown, 1998, p. 254.
60. Rubén Martínez, *Crossing Over.* New York: Henry Holt, 2001, p. 180.
61. University of California at Berkeley, "Some Illegal Residents Sent Back; Some Find Other Jobs," Agricultural Personnel Management Program news report, August 13, 2000, p. 1. http://are.berkeley.edu/APMP/pubs/i9news/differentproc81300.html.
62. Quoted in Jo Tuckman and Dudley Althaus, "27 Arrested in Smuggling Crackdown," *Houston Chronicle*, May 31, 2003, p. A1.
63. Quoted in Tuckman and Althaus, "27 Arrested in Smuggling Crackdown," *Houston Chronicle*, May 31, 2003 p. A1.

Chapter Seven: Living the American Dream

64. Quoted in Hammerback and Jensen, *The Rhetorical Career of Cesar Chavez*, p. 14.
65. Quoted in Mireya Navarro, "Trying to Get Beyond the Maid Role," *New York Times*, May 16, 2002, p. B1.
66. Esquibel Tywoniak and García, *Migrant Daughter*, p. 16.
67. Nobel e-Museum, "Mario J. Molina—Autobiography," April 8, 2003. www.nobel.se.
68. Martinez, *Mexican-Origin People in the United States*, p. xxi.

FOR FURTHER READING

Books

Beth Atkins, *Voices From The Field.* Boston: Joy Street, 1993. This book includes poems and photographs of migrant farmworkers' children.

Lawrence A. Cardoso, *Mexican Emigration to the United States 1897–1931.* Tuscon: University of Arizona Press, 1980. Looking at the first wave of Mexican immigration, Cardoso explains how conditions in Mexico "pushed" immigrants from their homeland, while the American need for cheap labor "pulled" them to the United States.

Julie Catalano, *The Mexican Americans.* New York: Chelsea House, 1996. This book for ages eight and up is a brief history of Mexican Americans, touching on some of the highlights of their experiences.

Susan Garver and Paula McGuire, *Coming to North America from Mexico, Cuba and Puerto Rico.* New York: Dell, 1987. This is a book in the Coming to America series that looks at Latino arrivals as the fastest-growing minority group in the 1980s.

Juan Gonzalez, *Harvest of Empire: A History of Latinos in America*, New York: Viking, 2000. This work traces the histories of Puerto Ricans, Mexicans, Cubans, Dominicans, Central Americans, Colombians, and Panamanians as they moved northward to the United States.

Dorothy and Thomas Hoobler, *The Circuit.* Albuquerque: University of New Mexico Press, 1997. A professor of modern languages writes stories of his childhood with his migrant family as they make the seasonal circuit.

———, *The Mexican American Family Album.* New York: Oxford University Press, 1994. With recommendations for further reading as well as a short timeline of great events related to Mexican American history, this book uses primary documents and family histories to present Mexican immigrant lives.

Francisco Jiménez, *Breaking Though.* New York: Houghton Mifflin, 2002. Jimenez writes stories from his boyhood as his migrant family is forced by the Immigration and Naturalization Service to leave their work site.

Jodine Mayberry, *Mexicans.* New York: Franklin Watts, 1992. As a book in the Recent American Immigrant series, it presents a brief overview of the history and people important to Mexican Americans and immigrants.

Carey McWilliams, *North from Mexico.* New York: J.B. Lippincott, 1949. This research is a standard in the field of Mexican immigration and the first book detailing Mexican American experiences in the borderlands up to 1948.

Wayne Moquin and Charles Van Doren, eds., *A Documentary History of Mexican Americans.* New York: Praeger, 1971. Beginning with the first arrival of the Spanish in 1528, this book uses primary documents to describe the experiences of Mexican-origin peoples of the American Southwest up to 1970.

Websites

American Experience (www.pbs.org). The PBS *American Experience* site includes information about the Zoot Suit riots as well as a timeline and music of the era.

El Teatro Campesino (www.elteatro-campesino.com). This site offers historical and current information on El Teatro Campesino and links to other sites.

La Prensa San Diego (www.laprensa-sandiego.org). *La Prensa* is a bilingual newspaper which views current events through a "Hispanic/Chicano perspective." Its archives include stories important to Mexican Americans and their history.

MAPA (www.mapa.org). The Mexican American Political Association site provides several relevant links to sites providing information on history, politics, publication, and other organizations pertaining to Mexican Americans. From here links connect to LULAC, the United Farm Workers of America, and American GI Forum.

National Council of La Raza (www.nclr.org). The National Council of La Raza offers a home page that links to various sites relevant to issues of importance to the council including policy issues, publications, and press releases.

Walter P. Reuther Library (www.reuther.wayne.edu). This library at Wayne State University in Detroit, Michigan, includes labor history and union archives. Audiovisual information and other exhibits are available online.

WORKS CONSULTED

Books

Robert R. Alvarez, *Familia.* Berkeley: University of California Press, 1987. The author traces the migration and immigration patterns of families living in both Baja California and the border region of the United States.

Shirley Anchor, *Mexican Americans in a Dallas Barrio.* Tucson: University of Arizona Press, 1979. An anthropologist moves to a Dallas, Texas, barrio to get to know the neighborhood and its people. She describes its rich life in her book.

Francisco E. Balderrama and Raymond Rodríguez, *Decade of Betrayal.* Albuquerque: University of New Mexico Press, 1995. The story of the repatriation of Mexicans and Mexican Americans during the 1930s is told in this social history.

Marilyn P. Davis, *Mexican Voices/American Dreams.* New York: Henry Holt, 1990. A researcher finds Mexican immigrants who agreed to tell their stories and explain their journey and struggles.

Arnoldo De León, *They Called Them Greasers.* Austin: University of Texas Press, 1983. This is a study of the history of racial attitudes of "white people in their role as discoverers, settlers, pioneers and landholders" in Texas. It looks at how whites felt about people of Mexican descent in the nineteenth century.

Sarah Deutsch, *No Separate Refuge.* New York: Oxford University Press, 1987. This work examines the struggle between Anglos and people of Mexican descent from 1880 to 1940 as whites sought to gain territory and power on the frontier regions of New Mexico and Colorado. It looks especially at the roles of Latina women within these cultural clashes.

Frances Esquibel Tywoniak and Mario T. García, *Migrant Daughter.* Berkeley: University of California Press, 2000. With the help of history professor García, Esquibel Tywoniak writes a memoir of her girlhood in New Mexico and California and describes her years in college and marriage to a non-Hispanic.

Ernesto Galarza, *Barrio Boy.* Notre Dame, IN: University of Notre Dame Press, 1971. This autobiography of a Mexican American scholar and social activist describes his early years in Mexico and in Sacramento, California.

Manuel Gamio, *Mexican Immigrant: His Life Story.* New York: Arno Press and *New York Times*, 1969. From 1926–1927 Gamio interviewed Mexican immigrants about their experiences and first published the collection in 1930.

Juan Ramon García, *Operation Wetback.* Westport, CT: Greenwood, 1980. This book, one in a series on ethnic studies, explains circumstances faced by undocumented workers who worked for American employers who exploited them. It describes the 1950s operation of the INS.

Mario T. García, *Mexican Americans.* New Haven, CT: Yale University Press, 1989. A historian looks at Mexican Americans from 1930–1960 as they tried to find their place in U.S. society. He examines leadership, organizations, and beliefs as they attempted to gain full access to American democracy.

Richard A. Garcia, *Rise of the Mexican-American Middleclass*. College Station: Texas A&M University Press, 1991. Examining San Antonio from 1929 to 1941, Garcia finds the variety of life experiences among immigrants and Mexican Americans from the poor to the wealthy.

Ramon Gonzales, *Between Two Cultures*. Tucson: University of Arizona Press, 1973. Anthropologist John J. Poggie Jr. records the life experiences of one immigrant.

Richard Griswold del Castillo and Arnoldo De León, *North to Aztlán*. New York: Twayne, 1996. This book is a well-written, comprehensive history of Mexican Americans in the United States for the Immigrant Heritage of America series.

John C. Hammerback and Richard J. Jensen, *The Rhetorical Career of Cesar Chavez*. College Station: Texas A&M University Press, 1998. Examining the speeches and words of Cesar Chavez, the authors suggest his complex understanding of his various audiences.

Jonathan Kandell, *La Capital*. New York: Henry Holt, 1988. An American journalist who grew up in Mexico writes a "biography of Mexico City."

Richard E. Lingenfelter, *The Hard Rock Miners*. Berkeley: University of California Press, 1974. This book is a history of the mining labor movement in the American West that shows the connection between the industrialization of western mines and the rise of the labor movement.

Oscar J. Martinez, *Mexican-Origin People in the United States*. Tucson: University of Arizona Press, 2001. Looking at the history, social progress, economic development, and the political participation of Mexican-origin people, this book finds patterns in their lives.

Rubén Martínez, *Crossing Over*. New York: Henry Holt, 2001. An award-winning journalist goes to the state of Michoacán, Mexico, and follows the lives of legal and illegal immigrants as they "cross over" the long U.S.-Mexican border.

Dionicio Morales, *Dionicio Morales: A Life in Two Cultures*. Houston, TX: University of Houston, 1997. This work is an autobiography of a young man whose parents fled the Mexican Revolution and who spent his boyhood in a small town in California during the 1920s and 1930s.

Raul Morin, *Among the Valiant*. Alhambra, CA: Borden, 1966. A descendant of immigrants tells of his World War II experiences and collects information on other Mexican American veterans.

Carlos Muñoz Jr., *Youth, Identity, Power*. New York: Verso, 1989. One of thirteen strike organizers of the Los Angeles school walkout, Muñoz looks back after twenty years to explain the events which began the Chicano movement.

Richard Rodriguez, *Hunger of Memory*. Boston: Bantam, 1983. This autobiography of an intellectual and journalist covers his early years as the son of Spanish-speaking immigrants.

George J. Sánchez, *Becoming Mexican American: Ethnicity, Culture, and Identity in Chicano Los Angeles, 1900–1945*. Oxford: Oxford University Press, 1993. This historian and activist examines Mexican American culture as it adapted and evolved in Los Angeles between 1900 and 1945.

Ronald Takaki, *Double Victory.* Boston: Little Brown, 2000. Written by a historian of Asian descent, this book is a multicultural history of America during World War II.

————, *A Larger Memory: A History of Our Diversity with Voices.* Boston: Little Brown, 1998. In this book, the author uses primary accounts of people of color who lived in the United States.

Elva Treviño Hart, *Barefoot Heart.* Tempe, AZ: Bilingual Press, 1999. This poignant autobiography describes the life of the youngest child of a migrant family living on the circuit.

Zaragosa Vargas, *Proletarians of the North.* Los Angeles: University of California Press, 1993. This history book describes the experiences of Mexican immigrant industrial workers in the Midwest from 1917 to 1933.

Periodicals

Barbara Bloom, "Cesar Chavez: His Fight for the Farm Workers," *Cobblestone*, vol. 10, no. 4, April 1989.

Grace C. Huerta and Leslie A. Flemmer, "Latina Women Speak," *Social Education*, vol. 15, no. 5, September 2001.

Jay Mathews, "Los Angeles' New Councilwoman Reflects Changing Ethnic Politics," *Washington Post*, April 14, 1987.

Seth Mydans, "Woman In the News: Gloria Molina," *New York Times*, February 21, 1991.

Mireya Navarro, "Trying to Get Beyond the Maid Role," *New York Times*, May 16, 2002.

Dial Torgerson, "Brown Power Unity Seen Behind School Disorders," *Los Angeles Times*, March 17, 1968.

Jo Tuckman and Dudley Althaus, "27 Arrested in Smuggling Crackdown," *Houston Chronicle*, May 31, 2003.

Internet Sources

Galán Incorporated Television & Film, "Chicano!" press review, March 26, 2003. www.galaninc.com.

Nobel e-Museum, "Mario J. Molina—Autobiography," April 8, 2003. www.nobel.se.

University of California at Berkeley, "Some Illegal Residents Sent Back; Some Find Other Jobs," Agricultural Personnel Management Program news report, August 13, 2000. http://are.berkeley.edu/APMP/ pubs/i9news/different-proc81300.html.

Websites

Galán Incorporated Television & Film (www.galaninc.com). This site describes films made of Mexican-origin people, including press reviews of documentaries about Chicanos including "Chicano! History of the Mexican-American Civil Rights Movement."

Nobel e-Museum (www.nobel.se). This site gives information on the Nobel laureates, including their biographies and speeches.

INDEX

About the Author

Barbara Lee Bloom grew up in California and graduated from UCLA. She received an M.A. from California State University at Long Beach, and a doctorate from the University of Vermont. She lives in Vermont and teaches history at Champlain College. She has written biography and historical fiction for young people, and her work has been published in the United States and Australia. This is her second book for Lucent.